Lettuce Pray

More Sermons from the Potato Field

Edgar (Ted) Stubbersfield

Copyright © 2016 Rachel Stubbersfield

All rights reserved.

ISBN: 0-9944157-6-1
ISBN-13: 978-0-9944157-6-9

DEDICATION

Dedicated to Barry and Elka Benz and the faithful team that turn up at our house for prayer every Wednesday night to seek the Lord that he might bring spiritual renewal to the Lockyer Valley.

Way back in 1972 Barry tried to teach me how to preach when I studied at the Church of Christ College in Kenmore, Brisbane.

CONTENTS

	The Farming Year	Pg # i
	Introduction	Pg# 1
1	The Devil was in Their Midst	Pg # 2
2	The Year of the Lord's Favour	Pg # 3
3	Silver and Gold have I None	Pg # 13
4	All Scripture is Inspired by God	Pg # 25
5	The Day of Small Things	Pg # 33
7	The Valley of Dry Bones	Pg # 45
8	A Vision for the Church	Pg # 54
9	The Spirit Filled Life	Pg # 61
10	Grace Mercy and Peace	Pg # 77
11	Walk With God	Pg # 85
12	Forgiveness	Pg # 88
13	Introduction to Daniel	Pg # 99
14	The Lord still Needs Donkeys	Pg # 111
15	He Can be Trusted	Pg # 123
16	Three Pictures of the Gospel	Pg # 129
17	I Want an E Type Jag	Pg # 139
18	Jobs Miserable Comforters	Pg # 151
19	Follow me and I will Give You That Farm	Pg # 164
20	The Parable of the Sower	Pg# 174
21	No Other Name	Pg# 184

THE FARMING YEAR IN TENT HILL

My first book of Sermons was called *Sermons From a Potato Field* because our little Baptist church in Tent Hill in South East Queensland, where the sermons were preached, is situated in the middle of a "spud patch". Because of this it is known as the church in the potato field. But in reality it is only a potato field for a few months of the year. The typical year could be:

Lettuce is a winter crop for us, planting starting at the end of March into July with the harvest six weeks after planting.

Potatoes was a spring crop but now planting can start in April and harvesting in early September to the end of November.

For a summer crop, vines such as pumpkin and watermelons are grown and harvesting starts in late November.

While the same crops are grown annually, there is a three year rotation between planting the crop back in the same field.

INTRODUCTION

Someone who was not a Christian picked up my first book of sermons and started to read it. Her comment was "I can understand this. Pity about the spelling and punctuation." Well, I have to plead guilty to the spelling and punctuation as I have dyslexia and getting the small points right is difficult for me but it was easily fixed with a lot more revision by others. As for expressing Christian spirituality in a form that can be understood, I sincerely hope that I am guilty of that too. You can be the judge.

I have included two sermons by other laymen in our church and a testimony of the Lord's saving grace and the gift of a potato farm to one of our number.

The sermons in the book are not organised in any particular order and were preached over a number of years to address a wide variety of situations. There can be no better outcome for this book than to say "I can understand this."

1. THE DEVIL WAS IN THEIR MIDST

The abduction of Daniel Morcombe on Queensland's Sunshine Coast is possibly the most high profile abduction and subsequent police investigation and later murder trial in Queensland's history. The convicted murderer had professed to being a new creation in Christ. This communion address was prompted by his conviction.

Reading John 13 18-30

We know the words of Matthew 26:28 well, "For this is my blood of the New Testament, which is shed for many for the remission of sins". But the passage from John reminds us that not everyone who sat around the Lord's table was forgiven.

We have been appalled at the depravity of Brett Peter Cowan since he was arrested and the more so since the trial and subsequent revelations, He was a man who claimed to have found God in jail and would have shared the Lord's supper week in week out with the saints. He was a devil, yet many of us saw him on TV talking about the new life created in him by a forgiving Saviour. It was all a lie, so big a lie that he might have even believed it himself. How do we make sense of it? How do the good folk at the Christian Outreach Centre in Woombye come to terms with the knowledge that a devil was in their midst for three years? How do the poor Morcombes deal with the anguish of such evil coming from one who would sit at the Lord's table and claim to been a new and holy creation?

The Lord's Supper reminds us that when his son walked the earth our Heavenly Father let evil men do to him whatever they wanted and it is no different today. Evil men everywhere would crucify afresh our Lord if they had the chance. Such evil need not be outside the walls but even at the very top of a church's government. The gospel is set before us, a broken body and the spilt blood, salvation that can be either embraced or walked upon. Let us embrace that salvation today but remain wise and thank God that the Kidsafe program was implemented with care.

2. THE YEAR OF THE LORD'S FAVOUR

This sermon was preached at the beginning of 2014 and reminded the good folk of Tent Hill that whatever befalls we will be living in the year of the Lord's favour.

Reading: *Luke 4:16-20*

[16] And he came to Nazareth, where he had been brought up: and, as his custom was, he went into the synagogue on the Sabbath day, and stood up for to read. [17] and there was delivered unto him the book of the prophet esaias. And when he had opened the book, he found the place where it was written, [18] the spirit of the Lord is upon me, because he hath anointed me to preach the gospel to the poor; he hath sent me to heal the brokenhearted, to preach deliverance to the captives, and recovering of sight to the blind, to set at liberty them that are bruised, [19] to preach the acceptable year of the Lord. [20] and he closed the book, and he gave it again to the minister, and sat down. And the eyes of all them that were in the synagogue were fastened on him.

Text: Isaiah 61: 1-7

[1] The spirit of the sovereign Lord is on me, because the Lord has anointed me to proclaim good news to the poor. He has sent me to bind up the brokenhearted, to proclaim freedom for the captives and release from darkness for the prisoners, [2] to proclaim the year of the Lord's favour and the day of vengeance of our God, to comfort all who mourn, [3] and provide for those who grieve in Zion— to bestow on them a crown of beauty instead of ashes, the oil of joy instead of mourning, and a garment of praise instead of a spirit of despair. They will be called oaks of righteousness, a planting of the Lord for the display of his splendor.

[4] they will rebuild the ancient ruins and restore the places long devastated; they will renew the ruined cities that have been

devastated for generations. ⁵ strangers will shepherd your flocks; foreigners will work your fields and vineyards. ⁶ and you will be called priests of the Lord, you will be named ministers of our God. You will feed on the wealth of nations, and in their riches you will boast.

⁷ instead of your shame you will receive a double portion, and instead of disgrace you will rejoice in your inheritance. And so you will inherit a double portion in your land, and everlasting joy will be yours.

This isn't the first time I had planned to preach on this text. The first time was in December 1972, and I use the word "planned" advisedly. I had just finished my first year in Bible college and I was left in charge of Gatton Church of Christ. I was preaching on the Sunday. I knew my text but strive as I might, the sermon would not come together. I have never had the same problem since, at least to the same extent. Mind you, this one almost beat again, every word seemed like pulling a tooth! I was too young then and probably too old now! There I was on Sunday morning with a text but no sermon. So I left for church with only the vague hope that the Lord would provide. He didn't have to; I never made it to church. On the way I had a massive epileptic attack, I was out for hours and, frankly, it almost killed me. Did my stressing about the sermon cause the attack or was I not able to put it together because the attack was coming on, I will never know. But it shouldn't have been the former. I learnt in later years that you can take any text you want and make it say anything you want.

2014 IS THE YEAR OF THE LORDS FAVOUR

Let's return to our text. The Spirit of the Living God may not be upon me, I may not be a living prophet but I believe I can proclaim to you today with certainty, as we enter into a new year, "this is the year of the Lord's favour."

If our Lord could proclaim this message of hope to those men attending the synagogue in Nazareth who, in a few minutes time, would be intent on killing him, I am certain I can say the same thing to the assembly of God's people who are longing for his return. This is the year of the Lord's favour. My friends, this is a message of hope to sinners as much as it is for God's saints, saints yet sinners. For them also, it is the year of the Lord's favour. "Oh Ted, now you are going too far."

Dietrich Bonhoeffer

You are just offering what Bonhoffer called "cheap grace". I know some of you are reading or have read his biography. It is a great read. He said in his book "The Cost of Discipleship":

"Cheap grace means grace sold on the market like cheapjacks' wares. The sacraments, the forgiveness of sin, and the consolations of religion are thrown away at cut prices. Grace is represented as the church's inexhaustible treasury, from which she showers blessings with generous hands, without asking questions or fixing limits. Grace without price; grace without cost!"

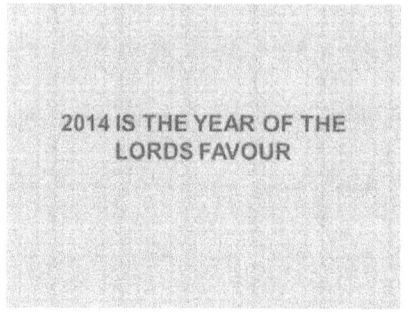

But no, I am just looking at the text. When you are preaching on a passage of scripture you should not be looking at what you want it to say (and plenty of that happens), but you must search out what it says but our text breaks this rule. Unusually, what is important here is what it does not say. Isaiah said to proclaim the year of the Lord's favour **and** the day of vengeance of our God, but Jesus cut his reading short and just said to preach the acceptable year of the Lord. It was not an oversight; he very deliberately rolled up the scroll at that point and handed it back to the attendant. It might have been overlooked by his congregation as they were not following with their Bibles open, but it should not be lost on us. What of God's judgement? Make no mistake, that day is coming but we are not the judge of the living and the dead. Until that day comes we are called to present and represent God's grace not just to sinners but to God's saints as we all fall short of our Lord's example. His message that morning was one of grace and pardon to people that did not deserve it.

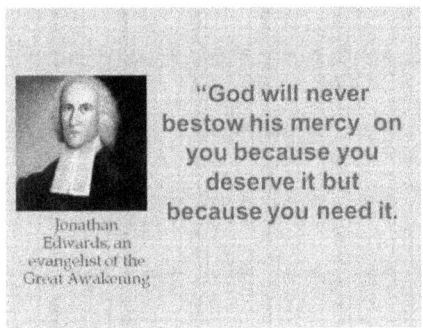

I am slowly reading another biography of Jonathan Edwards, the congregational minister in the Great Awakening in New England during the 1700's. This awakening was the first of a number of evangelical awakenings over the next 200 years. I suppose it is hard to shed the remaining vestiges of my Congregational upbringing. He taught that a man's will must be crushed with the law. He must know that he is a sinner destined for the flames of Hell. So intense was this condemnation and so difficult was God to find that he had to deal with at least one suicide.

Now, it has been reported last week that Hell has finally frozen over but I do not think that we can take much consolation from that. Grace and mercy was spoken to all but it is not a message that all will hear.

Good News for the Poor

Jesus said that morning, "He has anointed me to proclaim good news to the poor." It is not just the poor, that word is not strong enough. It is from the verb to cringe, or to crouch like a beggar. We have the same word in Matt 5:3 "Blessed are the poor in spirit, for theirs is the kingdom of heaven" and the same thought in Isaiah 66:2 "These are the ones I look on with favour: those who are humble and contrite in spirit, and who tremble at my word". These are people who bring absolutely nothing to God except their complete emptiness. As one commentator said "this is the condition and the attitude of true contrition for which the Baptist worked, on which he insisted and which alone opens the heart for the grace of the gospel so that he says of such "poor in spirit" that theirs is the kingdom of God."

What happened in Nazareth that day? Mark tells us in chapter 6 [4] Jesus said to them, 'a prophet is not without honour except in his own town, among his relatives and in his own home.' [5] He could not do any miracles there, except lay his hands on a few people who were ill and heal them. [6] He was amazed at their lack of faith. Even in such unfertile soil his ministry bore some fruit. I think we would be happy if we had a situation where, after preaching, some people responded with sufficient faith to be healed.

We all long to see an awakening in this valley, and with Reg[1] and Heather joining with Pastor and Mrs. Benz and ourselves on

---

1 A former elder and who along with his wife have been involved with the church for many decades.

Wednesday nights at 7 PM, to pray for that, hopefully that day will be a lot quicker in coming. In the meanwhile we speak a message of grace and pardon to a people, both saints and sinners, all of them people who do not deserve it. One thing Jonathan Edwards did realise and we need to realise, "God will never bestow his mercy on you because you deserve it but because you need it".

That day Jesus offered a message of peace and reconciliation to the poor and then gives three groups of people that trust in him will bring redemption, Those:

- Needing absolution
- Needing the sight of faith
- Needing release from misery

I doubt if there is one here that does not need help in at least one of these areas. It is only the mercy and grace of Christ that changes things.

For years, God had spoken through prophets, anointed by God. He had not left himself without a witness. But a man who was available, even a good man that was available was not good enough to be entrusted with this message of grace and pardon. Our heavenly father loved us so much that he prepared and anointed and then sent his own son with this good news. He would heal the broken-hearted, he would preach deliverance to the captives, he would give sight to the blind, he would set at liberty them that are bruised. Now this ministry, not entrusted to the prophets of old has been given to us. Go and preach the gospel, he told his disciples, to those close at hand and far away.

I have always had trouble with our Lord's words about John the Baptist, that he was the greatest person from the Old Testament era and yet the least in the kingdom will be greater than him. I know how the saints are often so imperfect and fail so easily and I have asked, "How can it be?" Part of the answer is in the difference in the message of grace and reconciliation given to us.

The year of the Lord's favour, or the acceptable year of the Lord. It is also called Jehovah's year of grace. The imagery in Luke's gospel is from Leviticus 25 where the Year of Jubilee is enshrined in Jewish law. After seven cycles of seven years, 49 in total, the fiftieth was to be a special year. Jewish slaves were freed, land was returned to its original owner and the poor who had no one to help them were singled out for special care. In the year of jubilee, those who had been dealt harshly through the circumstances of life were to be given a fresh start. This year was heralded in by the blowing of a ram's horn. That truly was a year of grace in a world that was anything but gracious and a picture of the restoration our Lord was to bring. But Jesus was not thinking about a year that came around every 50 years and not one that was heralded with a ram's horn but with a message spoken by God himself of mercy and grace. It was a year that came and stayed. That is why I can say to you that it is the year of the Lord's favour, just as last year's was and next years will be, if we are blessed to see it.

If we look at the whole passage in Isaiah it builds upon the Year of Jubilee and paints a picture of the return from exile in Babylon. And this was undoubtedly the first fulfilment of the prophesy but it was only a shadow. In the return from exile the whole nation was given a fresh start. Lord knows our nation needs a new start. Lord awaken the Great South Land of the Holy Spirit.

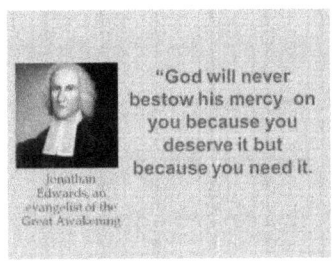

"God will never bestow his mercy on you because you deserve it but because you need it.

Jonathan Edwards, an evangelist of the Great Awakening

Every year the message comes to God's people and to those who should be his children, our Heavenly Father knows you need mercy and will never deal with us as we have deserved. Every new year the message should come to us "you can start again" in the words of Isaiah "⁷ instead of your shame you will receive a double portion, and instead of disgrace you will rejoice in your inheritance. And so you will inherit a double portion in your land, and everlasting joy will be yours"

Dr. Martin Lloyd-Jones

But let me return to cheap grace. Have I been saying that everything is rosy, God loves us and he will overlook everything? Ted you are making God's acceptance too easy, that's the old heresy with the big name of antinomianism. That is a word you will not hear very often. Well, if so, I am in good company. If I can quote Dr Martin Lloyd-Jones "if your preaching of the gospel of God's free grace in Christ does not provoke the charge from some of antinomianism, you're not preaching the gospel of the free grace of God in Christ."

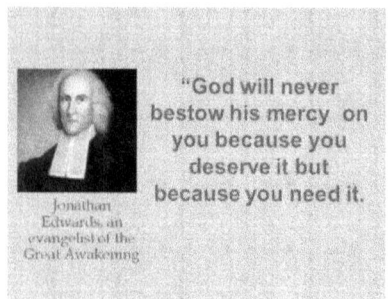

"God will never bestow his mercy on you because you deserve it but because you need it."

Jonathan Edwards, an evangelist of the Great Awakening

Grace will always be costly and discipleship will always be costly. But we have missed the point of our discipleship when no longer see that our Lord is far more willing to be gracious, and pardon our failings that we often give him credit. He is far more willing to meet our needs than we imagine, not because we deserve it but because he knows we need it. Jeremiah also foresaw the return from exile and his words to exiled Israel are also the words to us today as enter upon 2014.

This is what the Lord says: *'when seventy years are completed for Babylon, I will come to you and fulfil my good promise to bring you back to this place. [11] for I know the plans I have for you,' declares the Lord, 'plans to prosper you and not to harm you, plans to give you hope and a future. [12] then you will call on me and come and pray to me, and I will listen to you. [13] you will seek me and find me when you seek me with all your heart. [14] I will be found by you,' declares the Lord, 'and will bring you back from captivity*

Benediction

Rom. 15:13 - May the God of hope fill you with all joy and peace in believing, so that by the power of the holy spirit you may abound in hope.

3 SILVER AND GOLD HAVE I NONE

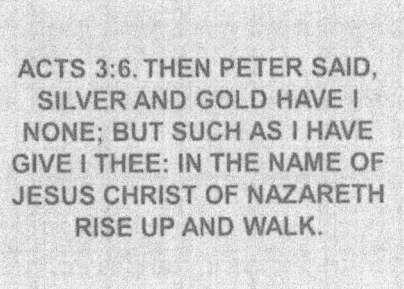

ACTS 3:6. THEN PETER SAID, SILVER AND GOLD HAVE I NONE; BUT SUCH AS I HAVE GIVE I THEE: IN THE NAME OF JESUS CHRIST OF NAZARETH RISE UP AND WALK.

Text: Acts 3:6

Then Peter said, Silver and gold have I none; but such as I have give I thee: In the name of Jesus Christ of Nazareth rise up and walk.

Introduction

After mulling the subject over in my mind for months I started working a sermon for the next time I spoke about a week before I left for Indonesia. Pastor Iain's illness has bought this sermon on earlier than expected.

NO LONGER CAN WE SAY "SILVER AND GOLD HAVE I NONE"

Sometime in the 13th Century, Thomas Aquinas, the leading

Catholic theologian visited Rome. He went in to see Pope Innocent 4th and the Pope happened, at that time, to be counting a very large amount of money. Pope Innocent said to him "You see Thomas, no longer can the church say, silver and gold have I none". Thomas made a very perceptive answer, "True Holy Father, but neither can she say rise up and walk."

Most Sundays I disappear into the back office to help count the offering. There are no great piles of gold but we are blessed with sufficient funds to pay our pastors, maintain our buildings, support local needs and send some away for missions. I am proud to be a member of this church and humbled by the trust you placed in me to be an elder. But like the church of the 13th century, here in Tent Hill, despite as Baptists having rid ourselves through blood and smoke of popes, priests and extravagant wealth, neither can we say "rise up and walk".

Are there miracles?

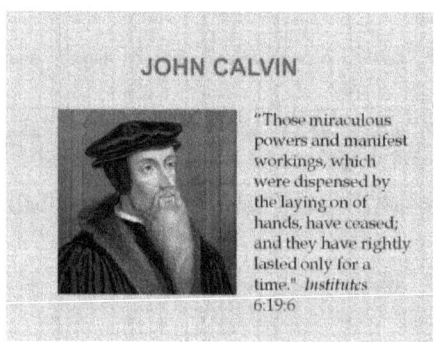

JOHN CALVIN

"Those miraculous powers and manifest workings, which were dispensed by the laying on of hands, have ceased; and they have rightly lasted only for a time." *Institutes* 6:19:6

When I was a young Christian there was bitter argument over the subject of miracles. If you believed that God was active in the lives of his people you were either a papist or chandelier swinging Pentecostal. Either way you were destined to the flames of hell. Calvin had spoken authoritatively in his institutes when he said "Those miraculous powers and manifest workings, which were dispensed by the laying on of hands, have ceased; and they have rightly lasted only for a time." How could they say anything different, their theology had to match their experience.

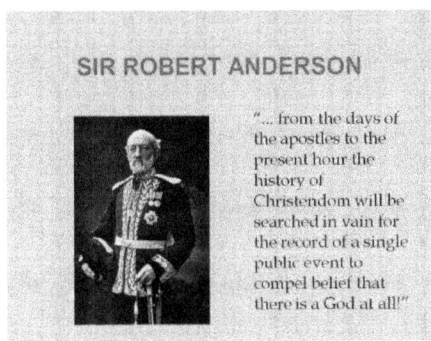

SIR ROBERT ANDERSON

"... from the days of the apostles to the present hour the history of Christendom will be searched in vain for the record of a single public event to compel belief that there is a God at all!"

They would have agreed with Ronald Anderson[2,] who wrote in one of the great works on suffering, *The Silence of God* (I am mentioning this book as it is a great book, still in print after 130 years, Tim[3], take the advice of an old man, you need to read this sooner rather than later in your ministry). He wrote:

"The mystery remains that God who at sundry times and in diverse manners spake in time past unto the fathers never speaks to his people now! The divine history of the favoured race for thousands of years teems with miracles by which God gave proof of his power with men, and yet we are confronted with the astonishing fact that from the days of the apostles to the present hour the history of Christendom will be searched in vain for the record of a single public event to compel belief that there is a God at all!"

Was he right?

---

[2] His other claim to fame is that he led the investigation into the Jack the Ripper murders,

[3] Our youth pastor

You probably have never noticed that, occasionally, in some of my sermons I have used a bit of poetic license with the truth. I am going to tell you a story and you are going to think, "He's doing it again", but it appears to be a true story. A mother living in the country looked out her window and to her horror saw her child playing on the railway line at the bottom of her property. The horror was that she could see a train approaching around a bend so the driver had no way avoiding the tragedy that had to happen. All of a sudden, out of sight of the child, the brakes went on and the train screeched to a stop just before hitting her child. There was no way the driver could have known. A miracle! Well no, the driver had passed out due to a medical condition and did not press the deadman button and the train stopped all by itself. Or was it a miracle? It all depends whether you view it through the eyes of a cynic or the eyes of faith.

Years ago I had to do an essay for a course and it was something like "What is a miracle"? There are so many definitions that it is virtually impossible to even know if we are talking about the same thing. If you walk away from a car accident, was it good luck, were the stars aligned correctly, was it random chance or was it a loving Saviour taking care of you. And if so was it providence or a miracle.

Did miracles really pass away with the death of the apostles? Church history is very clear that they didn't. Augustine, Bishop of Hippo, who died in 430 was the greatest theologian from Paul to Luther. His great work is the book *The City of God*. In it he talks about miracles. Augustine claimed to have personally witnessed two miracles[4] and as Bishop of Hippo he ensured accurate records of the miracles that occurred, in and around his diocese, were kept and publicly read and that his flock actively proclaimed their experiences. In two years over 70 miracles were recorded at one location alone in Hippo. A member of his congregation was healed of breast cancer and went to see her physician:

"When he had heard her account of what had happened, his voice and expression suggested, we are told that he thought little of it, so much so that she was afraid that he might make some insulting remark about Christ. But he replied with an air of humorous solemnity: "Why, I thought you were going to tell me something remarkable!" And when she looked horrified at this he hastily added, "What is so remarkable in Christ's healing a cancer, when he once raised to life a man four days dead?"[5]

After the children's talk we usually give them a sheet of paper and some pens. What if I were to give the adults a pen and paper too

---

[4]Augustine. *City of God* (Harmondsworth: Pelican, 1972) P. 1034 & 5.
[5]Augustine *City*...,. 1038 (Book 12, Chapter 8).

but instead of colouring it in I asked you to write about a time when our saviour had drawn close to you. Would you give back a blank piece of paper? What stories would your parents have written and your grandparents? I am sure we would have a book so stirring that none would deny that God has stood in our midst. Call these encounters what you will, I do not really care, whatever they are they declare that God's love for us is real. Personally I find it sad that these stories will be lost and the next generation will have to find out for themselves that their father's loving God is their loving God too.

One day I was sitting at my desk and as I looked at all the work that was in front of me I started shaking. I knew I was in trouble so I saw Dr John[6] and he sent me to see a doctor specialising in workplace stress and, after a few visits, the specialist then sent me to a psychologist. As we got talking about life I told him that I have trouble seeing anything except through the eyes of my faith, my successes and my failures. He said, "Don't worry, there are plenty like you." For many of us there is no random chance, through the eyes of faith, my God and your God makes the rain to fall (Matt. 5:45), he causes the grass to grow (Ps. 104:14), and he continually carries along all things by his word and power (Heb. 1:3). If he cares for his creation that way how much more must he care for you and I, his children created in his image and with his

---

[6] A former church member.

life in us. What was the doctor's advice? I had to make some positive lifestyle changes so I figured it was time to overcome my fear of spiders, so I went out and brought one.

Yet, somehow, most of the Christian church forgot that there was a loving Saviour who could be called upon in their time of need. I wonder how much experience drove their theology. But that was then and we are now.

BE CAREFUL OF LAPSED CONGREGATIONALISTS

John Alexander Dowie (1847-1907), a Congregational minister in Sydney had gravitas

As you know, I am a lapsed Congregationalist, as others of you are, Ross and Linda, Kylie too (I think). Congregational ministers in their Geneva gowns have a certain gravitas but never did I see one with as much gravitas as this man, John Alexander Dowie. The Australian Congregational Church has a lot to answer for.

BE CAREFUL OF LAPSED CONGREGATIONALISTS

John Alexander Dowie seen as Messenger of the Covenant and Elijah the Restorer

John Alexander Dowie (1847-1907) was a minister in Sydney. He was angry at the impotence of the medical profession during an epidemic which prompted him to study divine healing. Deaths in his church of about 150 people dropped from 20 to 30 a year to 5. Moving to Melbourne he attracted a number of people around him as he espoused healing.

He left for the United States in 1888, establishing a community of 10,000, near Chicago, called Zion City. Dowie suffered from delusions of grandeur and met with little success on a world tour in 1904. Zion City, and along with it his dream, would soon fail. But he made a lot of people think about God's loving care, many of the pioneering Pentecostals had their roots in his movement. But most did not look on him favourably. He ended up a ratbag with extreme views and his opponents could not see that there was a place for balance.

	All (excluding Catholic)			Christians Denominational differences among believers who have had such experiences			
	Most significant experience 1998	Change from 1991	% who have such experience often	% who have this experience often or occasionally	Anglican	Lutheran	Pentecostal
Answer to prayer in Unusual circumstances	17	>7	28	79	72	76	89
Through a specific call to action	3	<6	16	63	55	63	80
By deliverance from evil	3	n/a	17	61	53	64	75
Deep conviction of guilt over sin	3	n/a	22	68	58	73	85
Vivid mystical experience	4	>1	4	27	24	16	48
Miraculous healing	3	<8	4	25	24	25	45
Flow of daily life	44						
No experience	11	<11					

Fortunately the Australian believers no longer experience God's silence. By 1995, church statisticians concluded, encounters with God's power had become "a part of the faith journey of the majority of believers"[7] The present and growing reality of our Lord's intervention in the lives of his children is documented by the National Church Life Survey (NCLS) statistics as seen in this table. They show there is great value in encouraging expectancy and participation in prayer for the miraculous or whatever you want to call it.

---

[7] Kaldor, Peter, Robert Dixon, Ruth Powel and the NCLS Team, *Taking Stock, a profile of Australian Church Attenders*. (Adelaide: Openbook Publishers, 1999) 88.

	All Christians (excluding Catholic)			Denominational differences among believers who have had such experiences[8]			
	Most significant experience 1996	Change from 1991	who have such experience often	% who have this experience often or occasionally	Anglican	Lutheran	Pentecostal
Answer to prayer in Unusual circumstances	17	>7	28	79	72	76	89
Through a specific call to action	3	<6	16	63	55	63	80
By deliverance from evil	3	n/a	17	61	53	64	75
Deep conviction of guilt over sin	3	n/a	22	68	58	73	85
Vivid mystical experience	4	>1	4	27	24	16	48
Miraculous healing	3	<8	4	25	24	25	45
Flow of daily life	44						
No experience	11	<11					

---

[8] Extracted from Kaldor, Taking…, 89 and Kaldor et al, Views From The Pews, Adelaide: Openbook Publishers, 1995. 80-1. The question for the 1991 survey only asked what is the most significant experience. The 1999 data contained further questions as to whether the believer had different experiences. No later data is available.

I could ask, what is our theology here but theology and experience is not always the same thing. I remember an aging man who was an elder in a nearby church which he controlled with his wallet. His theology meant he was strongly opposed to any thought of our father's miraculous care of his saints. While in Manilla to meet his new bride to be, he had a heart attack. The doctor who was treating him said, "There is nothing I can do for you but I will pray for you tonight. Give me a list of all your ailments and I will ask Got to heal you". In a few days all symptoms of everything on the list were gone and he lived for many years afterwards. He told me that his only regret was that he did not make a longer list!

What is our experience here at Tent Hill. I went to the NCLS website but the report generated for our church did not have that information. I can't tell you what we as a group have experienced.

So what does this mean? We old Congregationalists have an adage "There is yet more light and truth to break forth from his word" But I am old enough to know there is no end to the darkness and deceptions that also call on the scriptures for their support. My friends, I believe the scriptures clearly teach that we can call on our Father when we are in need. There are some who will tell you that there are immutable laws that God must honour. Get the formula correct and God must answer our prayers favourably. They cite verses like Matthew 17: [20] He replied, "Because you have so little faith. Truly I tell you, if you have faith as small as a mustard seed, you can say to this mountain, 'Move from here to there,' and it will move. Nothing will be impossible for you."

If your requests of our Lord have not been answered the fault lies with you and no one else. At a men's morning barbecue fellowship, when I went back for seconds, I heard the two Pentecostal pastors bewailing the fact that God only seems to heal headaches and bad backs when they prayed but nothing remarkable. I piped in, "That, brothers, is because of your lack of faith. I know how Pentecostal theology works". When I once asked another woman I know how she was her response was, "Much better now that I have stopped going to church." She was conscious that she was being judged as lacking faith because she was ill. This belief that insists that God must act turns our father's loving care in our life from a blessing to, well I don't know what you would call it. You see, while our Lord says ask, he will not be commanded!

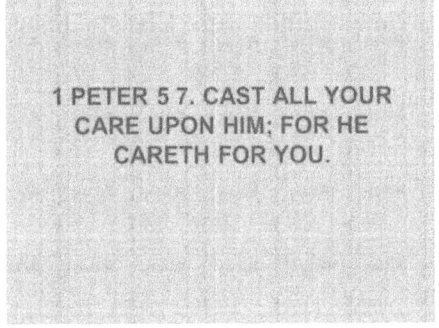

What can we ask of him and when can we do it? You know those verses verse from James 5 well [14] Is any sick among you? Let him call for the elders of the church; and let them pray over him, anointing him with oil in the name of the Lord: [15] And the prayer of faith shall save the sick, and the Lord shall raise him up; and if he have committed sins, they shall be forgiven him.

Do you have to wait till you are too sick to move to call on the elders or your brothers and sisters and then only when your health is the problem? What about "stress, discouragement, spiritual weakness, emotional weariness and fear. These are some examples of conditions that are not commonly defined as sickness, but nevertheless they are very dangerous, since they can be as debilitating and as damaging. In some cases and forms they can be more devastating than physical sickness to the individual concerned". I am certain that a whole range of afflictions that come upon the saints are in mind.

Finally, Peter said it all 1 Peter 5:7 "Cast all your care upon him; for he careth for you."

Benediction

Philippians 4:[4] Rejoice in the Lord always. I will say it again: rejoice! [5] Let your gentleness be evident to all. The Lord is near. [6] Do not be anxious about anything, but in every situation, by prayer and petition, with thanksgiving, present your requests to God. [7] And the peace of God, which transcends all understanding, will guard your hearts and your minds in Christ Jesus.

4. ALL SCRIPTURE IS INSPIRED BY GOD

This sermon was preached by Greg Sharpe, a friend, fellow Gideon and elder in tent hill Baptist Church. Greg is a petroleum engineer and businessman among other accomplishments.

Text: 2 Timothy 3:16

All Scripture is inspired by God and profitable for teaching, for reproof, for correction, for training in righteousness;

The focus of this presentation is the precept of Scripture being "inspired by God". We will start with the meaning of the precept followed by the resulting authority of Scripture and finish with the application of the precept to our lives. Before we start, however, I will briefly present the context of 2 Timothy 3:16.

Paul wrote his second letter to Timothy while imprisoned in Rome. He was expecting imminent execution:

For I am already being poured out as a drink offering, and the time of my departure has come. I have fought the good fight, I have finished the course, I have kept the faith;

2 Timothy 4:6-7 - NAS

The letter contains the last recorded words of the apostle, Paul. The words were to encourage and instruct the young Pastor in his ministerial work. Chapter three contains an exhortation to steadfastness during predicted apostasy and social corruption.

Verses 16 and 17 reinforce the power of the inspired Word of God to equip and perfect Christian workers for their tasks.

When Paul wrote the letter (in the original, Greek text) the belief in the inspiration of prophecy was widespread. Most of the Old Testament was attributed to Prophets therefore, like Paul, Judaism almost universally accepted the Old Testament as God's Word.

But what about the writings which were yet to be received as the New Testament?

As Paul wrote the letter he was writing words inspired by God. This fact is self-attesting but it is clearly confirmed by the Apostle Peter:

.....; just as also our beloved brother Paul, according to the wisdom given him, wrote to you, as also in all his letters, speaking in them of these things, in which are some things hard to understand, which the untaught and unstable distort, as they do also the rest of the Scriptures .....

2 Peter 3:15-16 - NAS

Paul was writing Scripture which Christianity would universally accept as God's Word.

In the preparation of this presentation my primary resource was the commentary, drafted by Dr R C Sproul on the Nineteen Articles of Affirmation and Denial produced by the Summit Meeting of the International Council on Biblical Inerrancy, 1978. The aim of the Summit Meeting was to bear witness to what the Council was convinced to be the biblical doctrine on the subject of the inspiration of Scripture. Parts of this presentation are quotes from the commentary which is readily available for download from the internet.

The following presentation is somewhat technical but as we start don't despair because it is also somewhat shorter than what we are accustomed to avoid your being presented with more information than what you can carefully consider.

A)- Theopneustos

With the context of 2 Tim. 3:16 in mind we will start with the meaning of the precept of Scripture being inspired by God.

The English word "Inspired" is translated from the Greek word "theopneustos" (theh-op'-nyoo-stos). Its root words are Theos meaning God and pneō (pneh'-o) meaning to breathe hard or to blow.

In the Amplified version theopneustos is translated as "God-breathed".

All Scripture is God-breathed OR, metaphorically speaking, all Scripture is the breath of God or from the mouth of God. Expiration is a more accurate translation than inspiration, with respect to the origin of Scripture. Inspiration, however, also conveys the part that the human writers played in the process of God's revelation to us.

Theopneustos is used only once in the New Testament and not used at all in secular Greek. These facts, along-with the fact that it was one of Paul's last recorded words, makes theopneustos an especially significant word. Dr N A Woychuck goes so far as to suggest that it "appears to have been fashioned by God for this supreme purpose of informing us accurately how the Word of God was transmitted into the language of men."

Let's begin to investigate the associated precept.

In doing so we encounter the phrase "verbal plenary inspiration" which is used to convey the concept that the whole of Scripture, not just parts, is inspired by God; down to the very words of the original text, including, for example, 'theopneustos'. This concept, however, does not infer that the mode of inspiration was dictation of each word by God and that the writers, such as Paul, were merely secretaries; despite some portions of Scripture (for example, the Ten Commandments) indicating some form of dictation. The key issue with verbal plenary inspiration is not the mode of inspiration but the origin of Scripture; that is, Scripture originated from God not from man.

"... for no prophecy was ever made by an act of human will, but men moved by the Holy Spirit spoke from God."

2 Peter 1:21 - NAS

Concerning the mode of inspiration, we are left with the question "Were the human authors passive instruments like pens in the hands of God OR were they not?"

The case for the authors being passive instruments is:-

1)- Inspiration overcame any tendency the human authors may have had to error with the result that the words they wrote were precisely what God, the divine author, intended us to have,

2)- Divine superintendence preserved the writers in their word choices from using words that would falsify or distort the message of Scripture and

3)- The writers were chosen and prepared by God for their sacred task.

The case against the authors being passive instruments is:-

1)- There are differences of vocabulary, style and literary structure amongst each of the human authors,

2)- The writers' distinctive personalities are conveyed by Scripture and

3)- These differences mean that God did not cancel out the exercise of the writers' personalities in the choices of words used to express the truth revealed.

It is therefore apparent that the Bible has dual authorship. God's part was to superintend the writing of the books, revealing His will. Man's part was to write this revelation using a human language and style so that God's message was preserved for generations to come. The Bible has dual authorship just as Christ has two natures. Christian theology maintains that Christ was fully God and fully human, the two natures united in one person.

"He is clothed with a robe dipped in blood, and His name is called The Word of God."

Rev. 19:13 - NAS

Christ is the incarnate Word; the Bible is the written Word.

Just as it is difficult to explain the divine mystery of the Incarnation, so it is difficult to explain the mystery of divine inspiration. In both cases God has given us revelation that is at both human and divine.

Through divine inspiration God made it possible for His truth to be communicated in an inspired way making use of the backgrounds, personalities and literary styles of these various writers. What is overcome by inspiration is not human personality, style or literary structure, but human tendencies to distortion, falsehood and error.

The Bible has a human dimension, in terms of authorship, but its humanity is transcended by virtue of its divine origin and inspiration. The precept of Scripture being inspired by God remains, however, a mystery. Contemporary theologian, Dr Erwin Lutzer, exclaims "Let us boldly confirm that God who became man is the same God who inspired common men to write a very uncommon book."

B)- Authority of Scripture

"All Scripture is inspired by God and profitable for teaching, for reproof, for correction, for training in righteousness; so that the man of God may be adequate, equipped for every good work."

2 Timothy 3:16-17 - NAS

".... profitable for teaching, for reproof, for correction, for training in righteousness; so that the man of God may be adequate, equipped for every good work."

Recently, I saw a sign (the same type that we have at the front) in front of the church with the words "Other books inform but the Bible transforms". What makes the Bible unique in this way?

Because Scripture is inspired by God it carries with it the authority of God Himself. Scripture therefore has the inherent authority to bind the consciences and to transform the hearts of men thus equipping them for every good work.

"For we are His workmanship, created in Christ Jesus for good works, which God prepared beforehand so that we would walk in them."

Ephesians 2:10 - NAS

There are those who will argue that the Bible lacks such authority because it was written by the created and not the Creator hence is limited by human language which is rendered inadequate by the effects of sin. I won't take the time this morning to present the argument against this claim but will simply reinforce what was previously presented, that is, the tendency towards corruption, distortion and falsehood by the human authors is overcome by divine inspiration and involvement in the preparation of Holy Scripture.

C)- Application / Surrender

During the introduction I referred to the acceptance of the Old & New Testaments as God's word.

Acceptance as an end in itself is information only.

Acceptance as a means to an end is transformation; hence the sign "Other books inform but the Bible transforms". When acceptance leads to the Bible becoming the authority for living out the Christian life the result is, by the Grace of God, the transforming conformity to the image of Christ.

It should be clarified, at this point, that the reference is to sanctification not salvation because acceptance of the inspiration of Scripture is not a prerequisite for salvation.

The most practical application of the precept of Scripture "being inspired by God" is reading with reverence.

Until I come, give attention to the public reading of Scripture, to exhortation and teaching.

1 Timothy 4:13 - NAS

Be diligent to present yourself approved to God as a workman who does not need to be ashamed, accurately handling the word of truth.

2 Timothy 2:15 - NAS

As an aid to diligent reading there are a variety of "Bible Reading Calendars" available such as this one published by "The Gideons International". I have a few with me which I will leave in the foyer for anyone who wants one.

Conclusion

As I close I will turn our focus to Matthew 26:53-54:-

"Or do you think that I cannot appeal to My Father, and He will at once put at My disposal more than twelve legions of angels? How then will the Scriptures be fulfilled, which say that it must happen this way?"

An escape from the cruel cross on Calvary was only an appeal away! More than 80,000 angels were at Jesus' immediate disposal; yet, He did not make the appeal! Jesus surrendered to the fulfilment of God breathed / theopneustos Scriptures.

"If anyone wishes to come after Me", Jesus said, "he must deny himself, and take up his cross and follow Me."

Matthew 16:24 - NAS

If we are His disciples we too must surrender to the authority of God breathed Scriptures with the consequence of self sacrifice, to some degree. The freedom we have in our country and community means that the degree will be lesser rather than greater but, we are not excused from knowing where we stand in relation to the precept of God breathed / theopneustos Scripture. Do you know where you stand?

With that exhortation in mind we will close this service with the hymn "Standing on the Promises".

"By the living Word of God I shall prevail – overcoming daily with the Spirit's sword - Standing on the promises of God!"

5. THE DAY OF SMALL THINGS

A constant theme in my reading and prayer has been revival. It is my hope that by the time I pass that I will see revival in my home church. Something remarkable happened in the Gatton Lutheran Church during the 60's and 70's but seemed to bypass the other churches. It encourages me to think it can happen again. This sermon was given to remind the church of our heritage as Australians and as German Baptists of revival.

Reading: Zachariah 4:1-10

*1Then the angel who had been talking with me returned and woke me, as though I had been asleep. 2 "What do you see now?" he asked.
I answered, "I see a solid gold lampstand with a bowl of oil on top of it. Around the bowl are seven lamps, each having seven spouts with wicks. 3 And I see two olive trees, one on each side of the bowl." 4 Then I asked the angel, "What are these, my lord? What do they mean?"
5 "Don't you know?" the angel asked.
"No, my lord," I replied.
6 Then he said to me, "This is what the Lord says to Zerubbabel: It is not by force nor by strength, but by my Spirit, says the Lord of Heaven's Armies. 7 Nothing, not even a mighty mountain, will stand in Zerubbabel's way; it will become a level plain before him! And when Zerubbabel sets the final stone of the Temple in place, the people will shout: 'May God bless it! May God bless it!'"
8 Then another message came to me from the Lord: 9 "Zerubbabel is the one who laid the foundation of this Temple, and he will complete it. Then you will know that the Lord of Heaven's Armies has sent me. 10 Do not despise these small beginnings, for the Lord rejoices to see the work begin, to see the plumb line in Zerubbabel's hand."*

Text: 1 Chron 12:23-32. *23These are the numbers of the men armed for battle who came to David at Hebron to turn Saul's kingdom over to him, as the Lord had said:*

24 from Judah, carrying shield and spear—6,800 armed for battle;
25 from Simeon, warriors ready for battle—7,100;
26 from Levi—4,600, 27 including Jehoiada, leader of the family of Aaron, with 3,700 men, 28 and Zadok, a brave young warrior, with 22 officers from his family;
29 from Benjamin, Saul's tribe—3,000, most of whom had remained loyal to Saul's house until then;
30 from Ephraim, brave warriors, famous in their own clans—20,800;
31 from half the tribe of Manasseh, designated by name to come and make David king—18,000;
32 from Issachar, men who understood the times and knew what Israel should do—200 chiefs, with all their relatives under their command;

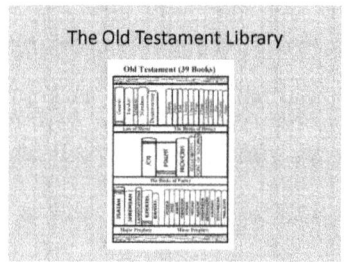

My friends, when I was a small boy in Sunday school I was taught that my Bible was not a book but a library. I remember a picture with the Old Testament on three shelves and the New Testament on another three. The library of the Old Testament was organised into the historical books, the poetical books and the books of prophecy.

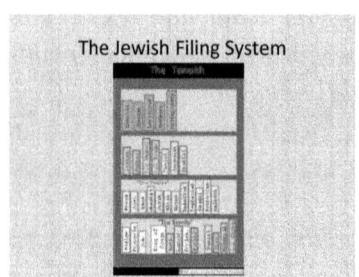

But the Jews arranged their shelves differently; they had the Law of Moses on one, then the prophets which they divided into the major prophets and the minor prophets and finally the scrolls or writings. What we might find strange is that Joshua, Judges, Samuel and Kings are classed as major prophets, along with Isaiah, Jeremiah and Ezekiel. Their history revealed their God to them. He was a loving father that could be known and intervened in their history for their good. They loved to retell God's great deeds, most noticeably in the Passover and in the Psalms (44, 83, 99, 106, 107, 114, 135). Even in the book of Acts, the longest message recorded is given by Stephen when he retells Israel's history. So, this morning, using God's word as our permission, I am going to use our church history to try and reveal something of God's nature to you. My aim is that, like the men of Issachar, we might at least in part understand the times and know what Christ's church should do. I am indebted to Drew for lending me Stewart Piggin's book *Spirit Word and World* on evangelical Christianity in Australia which made me think again on these things.

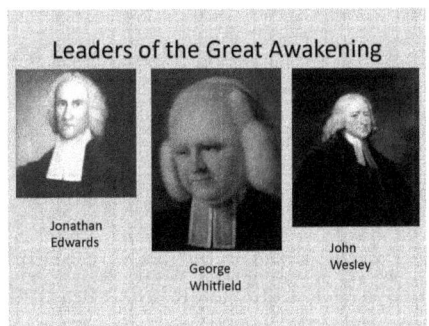

The birth of our English speaking evangelical heritage can be closely associated with the three leaders of the Great Awakening of the 1730's and 40's, Jonathan Edwards, George Whitfield and John Wesley. I have with me a biography of Jonathan Edwards and the journals of Wesley and Whitfield. Please take them from me and read them. They tell of a vibrancy and emotional involvement beyond anything we see in the Pentecostals, yet this represented the legitimate expression of mainstream Christianity and is our heritage.

The first ministers in the new colony, Richard Johnston and Samuel Marsden, were men grounded in revival and the writings of the evangelists of the Great Awakening. They had an expectation that God could move, but these Anglican ministers, from the sheer necessity of the infant colony, were men of divided attention which hampered their Christian ministry. Not surprisingly in 1794 Marsden wrote, "Almost all common morality and even decency were banished from the Colony".

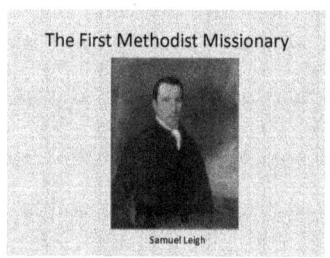

Australia was to receive its first Methodist missionary, Samuel Leigh, in 1816. Through a punishing work load, large circuits, and wise use of lay preachers he was able to bring the number of Methodists throughout Australia and the Pacific in 1831 from a mere handful to 736 communicants (church attendance much higher) and 14 missionaries. He would return to England that year with his health broken, but he would be replaced by men of like passions. These men had been described as the "Wesley's incarnate". They burned with a passion for souls.

The Push for Free Settlers
John Dinmore Lang

By 1830 Australia had a population of approximately 60,000, almost 90% of which had convict connections. The Presbyterian, John Dinmore Lang, realised that for a fundamental change to occur in Australia, free settlement was crucial as free settlers, not converted felons would be the backbone of the early churches. Through his nine voyages back to the UK he was able to foster immigration particularly from Scotland. But inroads were slow.

The first Chairman of what was to become the Queensland District of the Methodist Church sometime around 1863 described the evangelistic task ahead of them saying, "A force ... like an explosion of gun powder, and almost volcanic violence is needed to dislodge the intense worldliness of our colonial hearers". Is the task facing us any more daunting than the one that faced the early Methodists? Are men less unconverted? Is our Saviour less powerful? Is the joy of salvation less to be desired, can we now neglect so great a salvation?

Acknowledging that he was no Elijah, he pleaded to God for a revival. And revival did come, not a large national one such as we see in the revival of 1850's and the early 1900's in the UK and America but in a series of local revivals. Methodism in its various forms would continue to grow in Australia from virtually nothing in 1817 to 5.6% of the population in 1851 increasing to a staggering 13.36% in 1901. Overall Sunday school attendance was at 75%. As one historian said "One of the many stereotypes about Australian Christianity is that there has never been a religious revival in Australia. But revivals have actually been relatively frequent occurrences in Australian history." Are you aware that there were three relatively local revivals which were:

Warwick 1873
Toowoomba 1877
Marburg 1881

Warwick and Toowoomba

William George Taylor

The revivals in Warwick and Toowoomba are closely linked to the ministry of one man William G. Taylor.

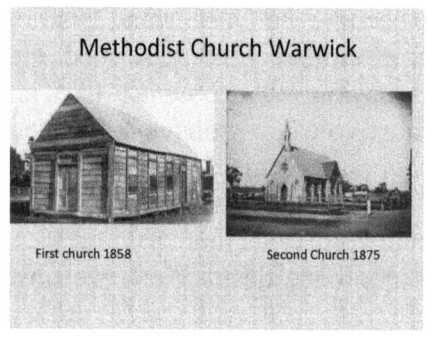

Methodist Church Warwick

First church 1858   Second Church 1875

By 1873, when the Warwick's population was 2000, the whole circuit could only muster 35 members (18 in Warwick) and 320 adherents. That year, the Rev. William Taylor was appointed to the Warwick church. On the first night "many were bathed in tears and ere we separated, eleven people came forward as seekers of salvation". The slab church was soon abandoned for the town hall which, in turn, was filled to the doors. He wrote:

"I have before me a list of the converts [127 names] of that time of wonderful visitation. It contains the names of quite a number of leading people of the district, many of whom have since put their impress upon the religious life of the community. After forty years that list greets me with the names of many who are still the forefront of things political, commercial and religious. I can furnish no finer answer than this to the quibbles of the doubters as to the permanent character of the results of revival work".

The Toowoomba church was little better. By 1876, when Taylor was sent to Toowoomba, the population was 6000, yet there were only twenty four Methodists on the roll. The church consisted of "a congregation of lovely people - intelligent, well to do, and alas contented ... too contented by far, with no response to the appeals for a forward movement that were made to them" (Taylor N.D.1, 107) . Eventually he persuaded the church to allow him to hire the School of Arts for one evangelistic meeting, There were 300 at the morning service and 500 at the evening service! He reports that there was no special evangelist or attempts at evangelism. He said of the revival that started to sweep the town:

"It represented Toowoomba's first baptism of fire. Spontaneous in its outbreak; natural , though rapid, in its development, its results were abiding. On my study table there lies before me a list of 135 persons who, within a few days were brought to God. I read that list today with a strange thrill of gladness. It contains the names of leading men and women of the town, who later on became buttresses of the church. Every section of the church was enriched. Our own membership was increased almost threefold, and at once Methodism took its stand as one of the leading forces of the Darling Downs (Taylor N.D. 1, 108).

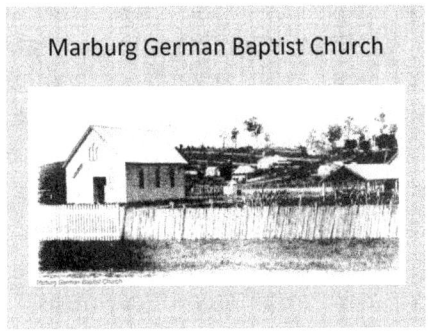

Marburg German Baptist Church

I can't tell you much about the revival in Marburg, the details are lost in an old computer system. But I did find in the Queensland Times 29th November 1881 "The Rev. E. Isaac, who, for a short time past, has-been conducting the services at the Baptist Church in this town, preached three farewell sermons on Sunday last-via., at 11 o'clock in the morning; at 3 in the afternoon, when the ordinance of baptism was administered to six female candidates; and at 7 in the evening. The congregations were large. That in the evening particularly so. On this occasion the preacher took his text from the 15th verse of the 24th chapter of Joshua--" And if it seem evil unto you to serve the Lord, choose you this day whom ye will serve," &c. At the conclusion of the service a prayer-meeting was held, and Mr. Isaac invited any of his hearers who were desirous of further information on spiritual subjects to meet him in the vestry after the meeting, A large number responded

Pastor Windolf at Kalbar

I asked David Parker, the Baptist historian if he knew of anymore and he replied "We suspect that there were probably many 'revival' type situations occurring in the German Baptist churches of that area during those years" I found in a history of the German Baptist churches, "Since 1904, Pastor Windolf[9] has resumed charge at Marburg. The six churches, with several preaching stations and three pastors, are now working harmoniously, ... The total membership is about 550, and, during the year 1905, a gracious revival led to no less than 75 baptisms.

---

[9] The great, through to great great great grandfather of many at Tent Hill Baptist church

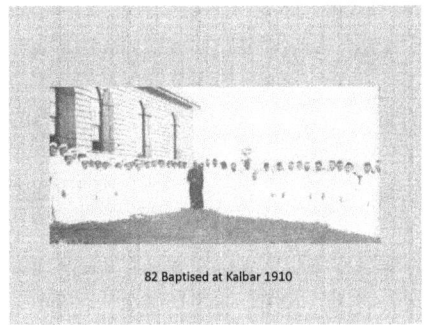

82 Baptised at Kalbar 1910

Another revival occurred at Kalbar in 1910 leading to 82 baptisms.

Now you are going to say "Ted, that was then but we are now". But Gatton in the 60's and 70's is not that far away. The Lutherans went from a small struggling and bruised church that could not attract a pastor to over six hundred communicants each service in a few years. It was unprecedented in the history of the Australian Lutheran Church.

My text commended the men of Issachar not because they were the best trained or the best armed or the biggest in number but because they understood the times. As in the days of Zerubbabel, we need to understand that we live in the days of small things but we can be lulled into thinking that because this may be all we have ever known then this is how it always was and it how it always must be. But that is not right. Our Lord said not to despise these days, certainly recognize them for what they are and to be grateful for and cherish every blessing. We are not to throw in the towel, not to stop our work of being Christ's light and salt in our valley. We must never think "I have labored in vain and spent my strength for naught" Isa 49:4.

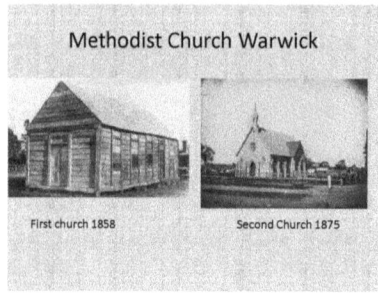

Methodist Church Warwick
First church 1858 — Second Church 1875

But the men of Issachar also knew what Israel must do, and what must we do if we understand these times? Well my time is close to being up but something must be said. But before I do that, I should say why we should seek revival. Is it just so that we can turn our slab huts into impressive stone buildings? Many of us have been blessed by what the revived Lutherans have built[10] but that is secondary. Primarily the saving work of many years is compressed into a short span and we ourselves are renewed and heaven rejoices.

The Right Application of the Right Means — Charles Finney

But how might it come? Charles Finney claimed that by the right application of the right means revival must happen. But all he left us with was revivalism not revivals, coming forward at an appeal without necessarily having a broken and contrite heart.

We live in a community no harder than that which the early Methodists found and revival did come in time. How does revival come? In Gatton it came unbidden and unexpected, In Warwick and Toowoomba it came through a very gifted evangelist. In Minden what we heard from the QT was preceded by the tragedy

---

10 This includes a primary and secondary school, retirement homes, aged care facilities and a remarkable ministry to the disabled.

of a boy being killed on his way home from Sunday school the week before. The great awakening was heralded by arguably the greatest philosopher America ever had in Jonathan Edwards and the greatest orator in the English language in Whitfield.

Yet this is not just the work of the elite. The 1857-8 revival in New York started when a simple layman Jeremiah Lamphier started a weekly prayer meeting for businessmen in the lunch hour in September, by October it was daily. Within six months, ten thousand business men were gathering daily for prayer in New York, and within two years, a million converts were added to the American churches …

The two big names of the 1850's revival in Wales were Humphrey Jones and David Morgan. Morgan, at first, was a sceptic but on hearing Jones speak was convinced of shortcomings in his ministry. At last David Morgan said to Jones, 'There can be no harm in our attempting to rouse the churches of the religion; I am willing to do my best. We can do no mischief by holding prayer meetings, though there should be no more than *man* in it all'. 'You do that,' responded the other, 'and I will guarantee that *God* will be with you very soon'. One night soon after, Daniel Morgan went to bed as usual, just a country pastor in a small town and woke in the morning and felt like there was a lion loose in him and just as suddenly left him two years later.

I can't point you to a method, there doesn't seem to be any. In many cases the unifying theme does seem to be prayer by those who long for change. What should Christ's church do? I repeat the words of the welsh revivalists 'There can be no harm in our attempting to rouse the churches; I am willing to do my best. We can do no mischief by holding prayer meetings, though there should be no more than *man* in it all'. 'You do that,' responded the other, 'and I will guarantee that *God* will be with you very soon'." Can you imagine if Pastor Ian woke with a lion loose inside him? More to the point, could we imagine if we woke with a lion loose inside of us.

Warwick and Toowoomba

William George Taylor

Revival is no panacea for the future. Where is Methodism? Where is Marburg Baptist church. Each generation must make the church relevant, But should our Lord visit us, in our older age we can be like William Taylor who said "At times I am tempted of the devil, tempted to think "I have laboured in vain and spent my strength for naught", … when the enemy of my soul comes at me with his "well circumstanced" temptation, and reminds me of the Prophets wail, "Who has believed our report? And to whom is the arm of the Lord revealed?" I just throw at his head the glorious facts of bygone days, and with confidence say to him, Now devil, what do you make of them".

May the Lord in his mercy break in upon us and take from us the days of small things.

7. VALLEY OF DRY BONES

Reading: Ezekiel 37 1-14

Text: Psalm 137

¹ By the rivers of Babylon we sat and wept when we remembered Zion.
² There on the poplars we hung our harps,
³ for there our captors asked us for songs, our tormentors demanded songs of joy;
   they said, "Sing us one of the songs of Zion!"
⁴ How can we sing the songs of the LORD while in a foreign land?
⁵ If I forget you, Jerusalem, may my right hand forget its skill.
⁶ May my tongue cling to the roof of my mouth if I do not remember you,
if I do not consider Jerusalem my highest joy.
⁷ Remember, Lord, what the Edomites did on the day Jerusalem fell.
"Tear it down," they cried, "tear it down to its foundations!"
⁸ Daughter Babylon, doomed to destruction, happy is the one who repays you according to what you have done to us. Happy is the one who seizes your infants and dashes them against the rocks.

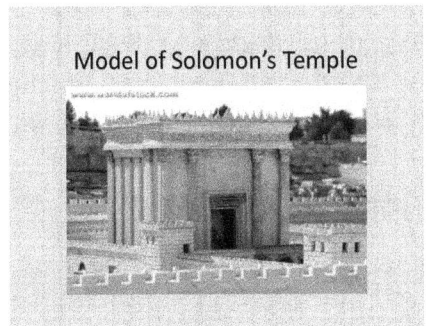
Model of Solomon's Temple

Introduction

Yahweh the God of Israel had chosen Jerusalem as the place to establish his temple and to dwell among men. It didn't matter much how the majority lived because the temple of the living God protected them, or so they thought. It would be their lucky charm and protection against any evil. God simply couldn't let his holy site be trampled upon by the ungodly. Their God had already been victorious over the gods of Egypt, and of Midian and of the Philistines and the Canaanites and the Assyrians. But these were no gods at all, just dead idols of stone or wood or metal. Surely, when Nebuchadnezzar came against Judah in 588 BC history would simply repeat itself. His god, Marduk, was just as dead as the other defeated gods.

Jerusalem fell in 586 BC

Some including Daniel and Ezekiel had already been taken captive but Jerusalem still stood and the temple with all its sacrifices, prayers and hymns continued. But after 30 months of unspeakable misery, fall it did and the army of Zedekiah was dried bones. The holy gold utensils of the temple of Yahweh were now being used in Marduk's temple, the temple of the lifeless god of the Babylonians. The humiliation of Yahweh was complete in the eyes of Babylon and Judah's enemies with the destruction of Jerusalem and its temple and the deportation of its citizens to Babylonia.

One of these captives poured out his heart in Psalm 137, without our temple, without our land, how can we sing the praises of Yahweh? The siege has been cruel and we know from the siege in Samaria how cruel that could be, as some parents even resorted to eating their own children. You can almost hear the cry "If the Lord will not help us, who will help us". Now the psalmist reflected the bitterness the exiles harboured against their captives in that they wanted someone to take their children and dash them against the rocks as would have happened to their own children.

We think we have problems to deal with, and everyone of us here has had to live with disappointment and sorrow. I am sure some of us have questioned "Why, Lord, aren't you helping us"? You know, you do not have to be in your box to be dry bones. Can bones such as these live?

God is in the Strange Land

Ezekiel, another Jew sat by a river of Babylon. It was 593 BC, seven years before the horrors that left the psalmist in despair.

Ezekiel 1 [1] *In my thirtieth year, in the fourth month on the fifth day, while I was among the exiles by the Kebar River, the heavens were opened and I saw visions of God.* [2] *On the fifth of the month—it was the fifth year of the exile of King Jehoiachin—* [3] *the word of the Lord came to Ezekiel the priest, the son of Buzi, by the Kebar River in the land of the Babylonians. There the hand of the Lord was on him.*

What follows is Ezekiel's attempt to describe the indescribable glory of the Lord. He wrote down a vision of living creatures and wheels within wheels full of eyes. But does God only see and not act? For a God who only sees but does not act may as well not exist. But this is not the God who has revealed himself in scripture and to us. When the slave Hagar in her extreme need met with God at the well in the wilderness she named it "the well of the Living God who sees me", when Abraham met with God on the mount outside of Jerusalem when he was about to sacrifice Isaac he called the place "the Lord, he sees". He sees your past, he sees your present and he sees your future, he saw the coming siege of Jerusalem, its fall, the bitter heart of the psalmist and the valley of dried bones and he sees your troubles and mine and he sees what might well be our church's coming financial struggle.

My friends, are you in a "strange land"? Perhaps you are walking a path you hoped you would never tread, perhaps you are faced with concerns about your health, or perhaps you are concerned about your finances, or a job or your studies. This is no strange land for your Lord, but one where his glory can be seen. He sees and he will act. Do you have deep-seated bitterness, and the circumstances of life can give you good reason to be bitter? Are there dry bones within you? Then the Lord's question comes to you afresh, "Can these bones live"?

Valley of Dry Bones

Valley of Dried Bones

Ezekiel in the previous chapter had been prophesying about the return of God's people from exile, a nation that no longer existed, a nation of dry bones becoming a living nation again. And his vision seems to be like a parable that reinforced that prophesy. And at the time promised the people returned and the nation was reborn. Some of us have lived long enough to see it born again in 1948. But if it is just about Old Testament history, politics and borders on a map it is of little interest to us, but it's not. In that chapter we read:

^{25} I will sprinkle clean water on you, and you will be clean; I will cleanse you from all your impurities and from all your idols. ^{26} I will give you a new heart and put a new spirit in you; I will remove from you your heart of stone and give you a heart of flesh. ^{27} And I will put my Spirit in you and move you to follow my decrees and be careful to keep my laws. ^{28} Then you will live in the land I gave your ancestors; you will be my people, and I will be your God. ^{29} I will save you from all your uncleanness.

No, this was not just a promise to the dry bones of Israel. This is a promise also to you and to me and to our children, and this is the promise of the gospel, the forgiveness of our sins.

John 3:3 *Jesus replied, "Very truly I tell you, no one can see the kingdom of God unless they are born again."* John 3:5 *Jesus answered, "Very truly I tell you, no one can enter the kingdom of God unless they are born of water and the Spirit.*

2 Cor 3:3 *You show that you are a letter from Christ, the result of our ministry, written not with ink but with the Spirit of the living God, not on tablets of stone but on tablets of human hearts.*

2 Cor 5:17 *Therefore, if anyone is in Christ, the new creation has come: The old has gone, the new is here!*

If there is one here who has not trusted Jesus you might say to me,

"How can that which is dry and lifeless within me live". "I have not earned it, I am not good enough, I don't have the inner strength to live for him. How can this be"? I asked the same questions back in 1970. Take your eyes off yourself, his all seeing eyes saw that about me and every person who names Christ as saviour. Salvation, the forgiveness of your sins is God's business. God wants to create something in you that was not there beforehand.

Not worthy! None of us ever were but God wants to raise you up to stand as a new creation. The message of turning from your sin must be heard, the message of repentance must be heeded but then comes the real message of restoration in Chapter 36 [37] "This is what the Sovereign Lord says: Once again I will yield to Israel's pleas and do this for them." But when you have trusted Jesus, the truth dawns upon you. He does all this because the all seeing God loves you, warts and all, with all your failings, past, present and future. He wants you to enjoy his friendship. Can these bones live? We testify to that fact.

Can These Bones Live?

You cannot imagine a greater contrast than the two visions of Ezekiel - the glory of God and the valley of dry bones, the everlasting glory and holiness of Yahweh and the death, humiliation and putrefaction of humanity. The question comes to Ezekiel, "Can these bones live?" What would the answer have been if the question was put to the psalmist? He had hung up his harp and could no longer sing the Lord's praises. What was his view of death – there isn't a clear Old Testament picture. We know of Job's testimony in 19:25-26

^{25} *"For I know that my redeemer lives, and at last he shall stand upon the earth.* ^{26} *And after my skin has thus been destroyed, then out of my flesh shall I see God."*

But in other places it portrays only gloom and despair with no hope

Psalm 6:5 *"Among the dead no one proclaims your name., Who praises you from the grave?"*

But Ezekiel had seen the glory of the Lord while sitting beside the same rivers of Babylon and he had the sense to hold his judgement and said "O Lord God, you know." What of your bones? What of the bones of those we love. We sang the dry bones song earlier and I remind you of its words "Now hear the word of the Lord. Dem bones, dem bones gonna walk around". One day the heavens will rend and the trumpet of God will sound and there will be a noise, a rattling sound, and the bones will come together, bone to bone and tendons and flesh will appear on them and skin will cover them. I do not believe this because of the vision of an ancient prophet. My Lord has gone before me, he has risen from the dead and he has promised to return for us, and not just us, there will be a vast army that will meet him in the air.

The Tomb is Empty

Just as Jesus commended his Spirit into his Father's hands he asks no more of us. Death is not a strange land for him. The grave with all the terrors that it held for the psalmists has now become sanctified by the presence of God himself. Can these bones live? It is no longer a riddle beyond mans comprehension. No longer need we say with Ezekiel, "God alone knows". All who have tasted the joy the dry bones of their spirit coming to life can boldly affirm, "Yes, because Christ lives".

Conclusion

The message of the valley of dry bones comes to us on many levels and has no single application. What of the dry bones of the Psalmist, were they ever healed? Of course there is no way of knowing but when time came for the return from exile, most decided to stay in Babylon, they were doing just fine. They had realised that they needed neither a holy land, nor priests nor temple. They developed the concept of the synagogue where even in a strange land; God could be worshiped and studied.

But many did return and the reformed nation did have a new heart. Never again did the lifeless gods hold the attraction for them that they had in the past. Amongst such people our Father could find ordinary people, upright in character and strong in faith, a carpenter and a young girl, who could be trusted with this world's most precious gift, our Lord Jesus. We see our news nightly we see how different the heart of Israel is to that of their neighbours.

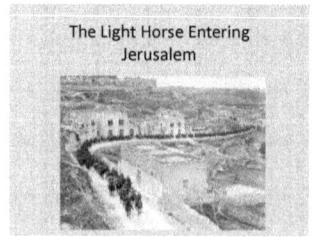

The Light Horse Entering Jerusalem

My uncle Bob was one of those glorious few Australian Lighthorsemen who liberated Jerusalem and raced Laurence of Arabia to the gates of Damascus. He was an active lay preacher before going to Palestine but never entered a church afterwards. He saw the wells in Armenian villages filled with the rotting bodies of Christians, murdered by the Turks. These bones cannot live he thought, and his own bones became very dry. You don't have to be outside the church to have dry bones that need to live.

The Sky, not the Grave is our Goal

And yet not all choose to disbelieve. Our Lord is still taking hearts of stone and creating in their place hearts of flesh, he is still putting a new spirit, his own Holy Spirit, into the hearts of men and women. There is a mighty army of his saints standing on this world now. Have you discovered his love for you yet? If you are feeling his stirrings, don't leave this place until you do.

Finally my friends, we know that one day we will meet the Lord in the air. Whether it will before we cast off this mortal coil we cannot know

"But Lord, 'tis for Thee, for Thy coming we wait,
The sky, not the grave, is our goal;
Oh, trump of the angel! Oh, voice of the Lord!
Blessed hope, blessed rest of my soul."

Though we may make dry bones, they will once again stand with those who are left, a mighty army, behind a mighty leader. Hasten that day Lord Jesus.

7. A VISION FOR THE CHURCH

The church was between pastors and I was not a member at that time. I was well known to the church through the Gideon's however and had preached there on occasions. Following a message a couple of weeks earlier about the pitfalls about appointing a new pastor, I was asked by Reg, one of the elders to speak about a vision for the church and how it might relate to the great commission.

Text: John 21:1-23

My text is the great commission in John, the acted parable of the large catch of fish. It is not my place to tell you what your vision must be but our text gives some direction on what it should be.

Imagine that the Baptist Union called in the same business management consultants that the banks have used, to deliver the gospel for the most cost effective manner in Gatton Shire. Surely they would recommend merging into one congregation, selling off the unwanted land and giving the money to the leprosy mission. It is only a short distance, you will do it for shopping, banking, why not the Lord? You would take him aside and say, "You do not understand, we are different"! His reply of course would be, "I don't understand, you are all Baptists, you all believe in the great commission, how can you be different?"

For Gatton and Tent Hill to say. "It is the Lord's will for us to exist as separate congregations", there must be a separate calling and purpose. A vision for this church, while it has the great commission at its heart, must also rise from what it is that makes you different. As you consider your vision it would be wise to ponder what it is that the Lord has built into this church over generations that make it different (not better). It is not likely that the Lord will draw a line under the past and discard it and start again.

Point 1 Some of your differences. I want to talk at the personal level, not as a church

Generosity

Through this church's donations to Gideons, I know this is a generous church. It is the big offerings that pay the bills and sacrificial offerings that make the church holy. Now these are not necessarily the same thing

Luke 21:1-4 *As he looked up, Jesus saw the rich putting their gifts into the temple treasury. He also saw a poor widow put in two very small copper coins. I tell you the truth, he said, this poor widow has put in more than all the others. All these people gave their gifts out of their wealth; but she out of her poverty gave all she had to live on.*

Not long ago I gave a large gift to my friend Noe in the Philippines to allow him to purchase a block of land to build a house. Now you are thinking, "I lost my reward by telling you". But there never was much reward as all my bills were paid and there was spare money in the bank. Ten years ago to give $50 would have been a sacrifice. For many the sacrifice is in giving our time and giving ourselves, like going to the prayer meeting when it is cold, raining, or being tired. There is a real danger that generosity can be seen as the vision, not the outworking of a vision. A vision cannot be bought!

Our text gives the clue to where a vision comes. [7]The disciple whom Jesus loved said to Peter, It is the Lord. To quote one commentator, "The beloved disciple, who, because he is closely bound to Jesus by love is best attuned to recognize him." A vision comes from years of walking with Christ, of hearing his voice, recognizing his ways, loving him deeply and knowing his love in return and countless acts of un-noticed sacrifice that show you can be trusted with a vision. The Lord has granted through this church's generosity the means of giving wings to its vision.

Missions support

The draft of fishes reminds us of the previous catch in Luke 5 where there was another miraculous catch where the net did not break and was followed by the call to be fishers of men. They left all, and the call to them now is again to leave all and be fishers of men

Jesus would give them a clear command in Matt. 28:18-20, *All Authority in heaven and in earth has been given unto me. Therefore go and make disciples of all nations, baptizing them in the name of the father and of the son and of the Holy Spirit and teaching them to obey everything I have commanded you. And surely I am with you even to the very end of the age.*

This church takes the command seriously but few have forsaken all. We must differentiate between vision and vocation, command and calling. I alluded to this in the introduction. There can be such an emphasis on missions that we fail to see our own calling, our own vocation. It took me 20 years to come to terms with it. A lecture from Professor Hans Schwarz on Luther's concept of vocation helped put it in place. To be a farmer, doctor, student, mother, businessman is a holy calling. It is as acceptable to God as being a pastor or a missionary. The problem is we compare our vocations, again we see this in our text.

20. Peter turned and saw that the disciple whom Jesus loved was following them (this is the one who had leaned back against Jesus at the supper and had said "Lord who is going to betray you?) 21. When Peter saw him he asked "Lord what about him". 22. Jesus

answered "If I want him to remain alive till I return, what is that to you? You must follow me.

As Baptists you hold to the priesthood of all believers, This doesn't say, "I can't speak in public so I will be a successful farmer so I can support missions" Instead it says, "My calling to be a farmer is a holy calling. I will serve God through my neighbour by growing his food, and providing employment when possible so he can purchase that food, I will master the calling of farming and be the best farmer I can be. I will show God's grace and love in the intimate sphere of interpersonal relationships. If the Lord prospers me I will also support missions".

The vision for the church must come from a complete acceptance of the holiness of our own calling and the confidence not to compare our vision and calling with that of others.

Point 2. The calling of the church

My AOG church has a vision or a mission statement: To implement the passion of Christ by making disciples committed to the unity of the church and serving the diverse culture of our city and beyond. Matt 28:19 and John 17:23. This is the vision of the ministry team, which it communicates to the congregation, which is supportive. This is a Baptist church and it is right that the vision is the vision of the church, which it communicates with the pastor. At your interviews you can and should say "This is our church's vision. Can you work with us to make it a reality". If he says, "No I have a different vision, a different direction", you need to ask. "is this the man?"

You need to avoid having a "Claytons vision",[11] the vision you have when you do not have a vision. "Our vision is to be a giving

---

[11] Claytons was a cordial which gave the appearance of being a spirit. Its advertising slogan was, "The drink you have when you are not having a drink".

church that strongly supports missions". That is not a vision, it is a statement of who you are. A true vision must be an object of faith, something perceived but not yet in your grasp. To see something from a distance and welcome it. There will be two aspects to this church receiving a real vision

Sacrifice – sacrifice is always directed to the future. It is seen as something that is worth giving up a Wednesday night for; and

Contentment – contentment with our own calling, not just personally, but as a church, content that this church will be different. It is not your worry if there are bigger, more generous, missionary minded churches. Praise God for such a church, but we have been called to walk this way

Point 3 Believing God for an effective vision

In verse three we see aimless activity undertaken in desperation and it is unsuccessful because it is without Jesus. (John 15:5 Apart from me you can do nothing.) But when Jesus comes and he blesses, the morning catch is miraculous even though they normally fished at night.

There is not much difference between complete failure and the supernatural success. It was not changing bait, nor changing tackle. It was not changing methods or how they held their mouth. It was just going from the left hand to the right hand of boat! From left hand without him to right hand with him.

What about the supernatural? I first spoke in tongues in 1970 and there was only one explanation, I had a demon. There is now a 51% chance your new pastor will speak or approve of speaking in tongues. Now I am not suggesting you become Pentecostals if that is how you define people who speak in tongues. Did you know that 37% of you are there already?

There is a willingness to look beyond the day of small things - despise not the day of small things - but we need to recognize it for what it is

Some statistics about Baptists

84% often or occasionally had an answer to prayer in unusual circumstances
73% often or occasionally had a specific call to action
20% often or occasionally had a miraculous healing
65% often or occasionally had a deliverance from evil
25% often or occasionally had a vivid mystical experience

In the Baptist statistics there are none who had not encountered the reality of God in a supernatural way yet 11% of Christians outside have not. As individuals you have experienced God's power in your midst. (An example of the remarkable conversion of Reg's the father was mentioned). If someone was sick and called for the elders wouldn't you come? You have every reason to believe that this power can be experienced as a church.

How did you as individuals experience it? By prayer. How will you as a church experience it? By corporate prayer. United like the Jerusalem church in Acts. You don't need the pastor's approval. As Baptists you can say, "I do not know what you are doing on Wednesday night pastor but we are having a church prayer meeting and you are welcome to come," I am talking about revival. You have heard about it, and you have read about it. Don't you want to see it. Barry Benz[12] and I met for prayer for revival for two years, and he saw solid growth in his church but no revival. I was fortunate to see it at Pensacola. For two years the church prayed beforehand. It can happen at Tent Hill, do you want it to happen?

---

12 Pastpr of Gatton church of Christ who tried to teach me to preach in 1972.

We get back to the matter of sacrifice, to the farmer who should be in bed after an early morning and a hard day. To mothers who have to care for young children, I would ask you to meet faithfully for two years to pray for God's power to be seen.

Conclusion

It is better not to grasp a vision than to grasp it without courage. In Luke 7:30 The Pharisees and the Lawyers rejected God's will for themselves. The passage explains why in verse 47 "To whom little is forgiven, the same loves little". There is a danger in a church of second generation Christians that they love little.

In our text the net was not torn, today few care if the net is torn and the catch escapes. It was easy in the past to let those views that I held be a cause of division. To speak about the great commission and despise the unity of the faith.

May God grant you a vision worthy of a powerful God, the sacrifice to see it through to reality, the contentment in your calling, the courage not to reject it and the wisdom not to tear the net.

8. THE SPIRIT FILLED LIFE

A far longer time ago than I care to admit, I first started to study theology in a Church of Christ College in Brisbane. One day a student rushed late into devotions and, as he opened up his Bible, he saw that in his haste he had grabbed an old one from off the desk where he had been working. That Bible had bits cut out of it. The lecturer spotted this sacrilege and queried it in front of everyone. The hapless student's quick reply was that "I didn't agree with those bits". So Australian humour is an acquired taste, but to my ears it is a better answer than the truth. That was in the days long before word processors and he simply cut the passages out to stick in his assignments.

If we could see another person's Bible, as they see it, probably we would find bits at least cut out mentally and other portions with heavy underlining. The portions they either ignored or at least were not comfortable with and the bits they loved. I'm guilty too and wish I could take the scissors to certain passages in the Psalms. For many, the passages dealing with the Gifts are the Spirit receive either the mental scissors or highlighter treatment. Even though Luther would have liked to have taken the scissors to the Epistle of Straw, James, he resisted the temptation and the scissors brigade must do likewise. Similarly, the highlighter mob needs to take an eraser to the markings on their favourite texts and not give them undue emphasis.

I named Christ as mine in 1970 meaning I'm old enough to recall the bitter divisions that existed over the Holy Spirit. In Australia there were very few Pentecostals and the lines were drawn firmly between those who had the Baptism in the Spirit, "the fullness of the Holy Spirit" as they described it and those who did not. It was not just disapproval, or lack of interest but hostility, even a blind hatred. With the Charismatic Renewal just starting to gain momentum in Brisbane the boundaries initially became even more sharply delineated. In my own home town, removed from the developments in Brisbane, the prevailing view among evangelicals was that Pentecostals had a demon. On the other side of the coin, The "Pentes" considered that the evangelicals just didn't quite have all of the Spirit.

To be perfectly honest, both sides gave each other plenty of ammunition. In Australia, the Pentecostals were seen as having extreme practices and, due to the moral failings of a very prominent pioneering evangelist, were portrayed as tolerating immorality. One old AOG pioneer described the attitude saying, "it wasn't opposition, it was persecution". On the other side there could be little life in the mainstream churches and they were being deserted in droves. It all boiled down to this. One side claimed to be living the Spirit filled life with the initial evidence of the Baptism in the Holy Spirit being the ability to speak in tongues with charismatic gifts following. On the other side, they were convinced that all the gifts had ceased with the death of the last apostle. All that a Christian could hope to produce was the fruit of the Spirit. God was now quiet. But the Christian community has changed since then. Half don't care either way and slightly more approve than disapprove and it is questionable how seriously most of those disapprove. God is no longer silent in Australia. By 1995, church statisticians concluded, encounters with God's power had become "a part of the faith journey of the majority of believers". On the downside, with "respectability" I fear the Pentecostals are generally lacking powerful preachers of God's word that they once had. Perhaps as a consequence many are flocking to the latest new thing, the missing ingredient, so that they might indeed finally walk on water.

Discussing the Spirit Filled Life, a life claimed to lived above the level above others through Spirit given gifts takes us straight into the mine field of the two opposing camps, of Gifts of the Spirit verses the Fruit of the Spirit. Perhaps it is a little dangerous to hear what a lapsed, though still sympathetic Pentecostal says about such things. But bear with me to the end and most of us from both sides of the divide will part as friends. This issue divided the church for too long, but now it seems almost anything is acceptable and it troubles my poor old heart that too often the church has lost the power and ability to know and to declare that things aren't right.

The Gifts of the Spirit 1 Cor. 12:8-10	
1	Speak with wisdom
2	Speak with knowledge
3	Faith
4	Gifts of healing
5	Miraculous powers
6	Prophecy
7	Distinguishing spirits
8	Different tongues
9	Interpreting tongues

So let's throw caution to the wind and start with the Gifts of the Spirit. We are all probably well enough acquainted with this list and some of us might be a bit uncomfortable seeing some of these things happen in our church. They are a bit "out there". (Mind you some of our Pentecostal brothers and sisters might be just as glad to see them again I have observed that in Australia at least the way you tell a Baptist from most Pentecostal churches, in its services at least, is from the sign outside).

Could you imagine having a prophet in your midst like the prophet Agabus. I don't know what we would say if he got up in our little country Baptist Church in, Queensland and prophesied as he did in Acts 11:28 saying "There is going to be a drought in the Lockyer Valley". Well, there would not be too many prizes for getting that right; our creek did not run for ten years in the last drought! I don't think we would be too upset if there was someone with the gift of healing as even the staid Anglicans have the Order of St. Luke. Unless you are seeking miracles for entertainment, nothing sees a miracle but despair, pain and sickness and there would be no church without its share of heartache and misery. But the reality is that we don't see the things we want to see and we must witness things we don't want to see. I expect for most churches the attitude would be, "Lord we will have all this but we will have it without tongues, thank you."

12:8-10	12:28	12;29-30
Speak with wisdom	Apostles	Apostles
Speak with knowledge	Prophets	Prophets
Faith	Teachers	Teachers
Gifts of healing	Miracle workers	Miracle workers
Miraculous powers	Healing gifts	Gifts of healing
Prophecy	Helping others	Different tongues
Distinguishing spirits	Administration	Interpreting tongues
Different tongues	Different tongues	
Interpreting tongues		

13:1-3	14:6	14:26
Different tongues	Different tongues	Hymn
prophecy	Revelation	Revelation
Knowledge of mysteries	Knowledge	Word of instruction
Faith	Prophecy	Tongue
Give all I possess	Teaching	Interpretation
Surrender my body		

So there are nine Gifts of the Spirit? Well you don't have to be reading your Bible very long to realise that nothing is as simple as that. Rather than one list of gifts in 1 Corinthians, I can find six lists.

Now a practicing Pentecostal will look at these lists and say "See I told you tongues were important. There they are in every list". They have a point and we should not be too critical if they broke out into "Oh for a thousand tongues". What would save us is that Australian Pentecostals don't sing hymns any longer and would not know the words.

I look at the same list very differently. Here I have put a number beside each gift as it is first listed and used that same number whenever the gift is repeated. I find seventeen gifts. Agreed, some of these gifts are difficult to distinguish from others and you might get only sixteen or fifteen, but whatever it is, it will be a lot more than nine.

	12:8-10		12:28		12;29-30
1	Speak with wisdom	10	Apostles	10	Apostles
2	Speak with knowledge	6	Prophets	12	Prophets
3	Faith	11	Teachers	11	Teachers
4	Gifts of healing	5	Miracle	5	Miracle
5	Miraculous powers	4	Healing gifts	4	Gifts of healing
6	Prophecy	12	Helping others	8	Different
7	Distinguishing spirits	13	Administration	9	Interpreting tongues
8	Different tongues	8	Different tongues		
9	Interpreting tongues				
	13:1-3		**14:6**		**14:26**
8	Different tongues	8	Different	16	Hymn
6	prophecy	2	Revelation	11	Revelation
2	Knowledge of mysteries	2	Knowledge	17	Word of instruction
3	Faith	6	Prophecy	8	Tongue
14	Give all I possess	11	Teaching	9	Interpretation
15	Surrender my body				

"But wait, there is more" as the telemarketers say, there is another gift. In 1 Corinthians 7:7 where we learn of the gift of celibacy. Personally I would prefer the steak knives! Strange, but I never heard a young man pray for that gift. I did hear a young woman pray it once. (Not a prayer I wanted to hear as we were keeping company). I understand that if you want to hear this prayer you must visit the Catholic seminaries. There has probably not been a more honest if not entirely spiritual prayer than that of St Augustine, "Lord Grant me chastity, but not yet."

14	Give all I possess
15	Surrender my body

Look at gifts fourteen and fifteen, giving away everything we have and giving our bodies to the flames. I have never seen either of these and I hope never to see anyone burn, but a pastor we support, who lives near the border of Orissa India, sent me images of Christians burnt by the Hindus in that state. The pictures are heart wrenching. Our little church has also had a long association with Graham Staines and the Evangelical Missionary Society of Mayurbhanj renowned for its work with lepers in Orissa. We were devastated when we heard that he and his two sons had been burnt to death in their vehicle in that state.

But I Corinthians 13:1-3 questions whether these things have any value to a person without love. I have stood very briefly at the spot in Broad Street, Oxford where the reforming bishops Latimer and Ridley and later Archbishop Cranmer, the Oxford Martyrs, were burnt alive. It was only briefly as it is in the middle of the road. Latimer and Ridley were burned together on October 16, 1555. Latimer's alleged words to Ridley as they waited for the flames to consume them are stirring even today, "Be of good cheer and play the man, Master Ridley; we shall this day light such a candle, by God's grace, in England, as I trust shall never be put out." Their place in Anglican reverence was firmly established that day.

But the Baptists viewed things very differently. They were not impressed and they were not sympathetic. In effect they said "Don't look to us for sympathy. You clapped your hands when Elizabeth and Mary burnt Baptists". Most of them were probably ordinary people like you and me. Latimer and Ridley gave their bodies to the flames but where was their love? To love our Lord more than life itself and to be so moved by compassion that your generosity knows no bounds are gifts of the Spirit that have not passed away. They are gifts that will grab attention far more than someone who can stand up in a service and speak unintelligible words. The truly remarkable Gifts of the Spirit have not passed away and may he pour out this spirit upon his church in even greater measure.

11	Teachers
12	Helping Others
13	Administration
16	Hymns
17	Word of Instruction

Look at the next group, teaching, helping others, administration, hymns and, word of instruction. These are as ordinary as the last two were extraordinary. I'm only a deacon in this church and have never attended an elders meeting. Perhaps they huddle round in a circle and Pastor Ian says to them, "When we start to feel the Spirit descend on us and we start to shake, we will be about the Lord's business of administration". (This is extreme I know, but it has happened in church history). Of course this is not how it works, at least I hope not. What I expect happens in my church and yours is that someone prays, someone does a devotion and then they get down to the business of administration. Yet if the gift of administration is not present, hidden in the very ordinariness of the evening's proceedings, my church and yours would not be administered well.

Did you notice that in Paul's list he had hymns? (Just a tongue in cheek reminder, he said hymns, not choruses or Hillsong). Let me digress for a while. I once knew a minister who also had a Christian music ministry. He told me how one Australian songwriter/recording artist received $200,000 in royalty from one song and commented "I would like to do that". Wouldn't we all! Or would we? It brings into question the thorny issue of taking money from a God given gift. Martin Luther's publisher became a rich man from Martin's books but the reformer himself refused to take any royalties. But a man must live so he, or more correctly his wife started a brewery and established an inn in the old Augustinian monetary that was given to him. Now many in my little Baptist church with a German heritage would probably say "and the problem is"? A Methodist would have been appalled and would probably have counselled him that it was better to have taken the royalty. But I have been digressing along a particularly difficult path. As a wise man once said "The Lord put a new song in my heart until copyright law took it away."

The gifts have all passed away I have been told, I hope the gift of new songs and music with which to praise our God hasn't. What about the gift of helping others? We saw this in abundance when an inland tsunami ripped through our peaceful valley in January 2010 taking some to their death and destroying the hopes and livelihood of many. No thinking person could have said that the churches were irrelevant. The people of this group are all very ordinary. You would struggle to see the Spirit in this group, yet, probably this is where the Spirit is most at work.

So God has gifted his church with seventeen gifts and seventeen gifts only and an anathema on all who say there are fewer or more than seventeen! Surely not! Are these seventeen gifts meant to be an exhaustive or a representative list. Surely the Gifts of the Spirit to the church are without number? More likely the understanding should be that the church need never face a situation that is beyond the help of the Spirit that gives gifts to His church without measure. Perhaps we need to recognise how willing the Lord is to give gifts to His church.

The fruit of the Spirit	
1	Love
2	Joy
3	Peace
4	Patience
5	Kindness
6	Goodness
7	Faithfulness
8	Gentleness
9	Self Control

"This talk about gifts is all very well and good" you might say, but Paul did say that he would show us the more excellent way of faith, hope and Love (1 Cor 12:31 – 13:13). In the end it has to be about the Fruit of the Spirit because love is a Fruit of the Spirit. And we know these fruit well. There are another eight besides love.

But again the messages of the telemarketers come to us, "But wait, there's more". We should know by now that it is never that simple. Paul gives us another list of the Fruit of the Spirit in Colossians 3:12-14.

The fruit of the Spirit Gal 5:22-3		The fruit of the Spirit Col 3:12-14	
1	Love	10	Compassion
2	Joy	5	Kindness
3	Peace	11	Humility
4	Patience	8	Gentleness
5	Kindness	4	Patience
6	Goodness	12	Forbearing
7	Faithfulness	13	Forgiving
8	Gentleness	1	Loving
9	Self Control		

Go through them, I count thirteen Fruit of the Spirit. Do we have an exhaustive list, thirteen and no more? Surely not! Where is graciousness in either list but it has to be included. Surely the Fruit of the Spirit must be without number like his gifts. Paul does not say "Against *these* things there is no law" but "against *such* things".

What can we say about the Fruit of the Spirit? Their essential nature is that they reproduce the life of Christ in the believer. It is hardly surprising that the words in the list are in the Gospels of Christ. We aren't just to learn about Christ but to learn *Him*. We do this by putting off what Paul calls the "old nature", just like an old piece of clothing (Col 3:9-10) and taking on His nature. This process we call this the Fruit of the Spirit.

Now some out there might say, "Ted, that is just how I like it, I want to be like Jesus. Leave all that contentious miraculous stuff behind and give me a nice set of rules that I can line my actions against to see how my life measures up". But Christ's nature is not about rules; it is about walking in the Spirit, and being led by the Spirit and the Spirit producing fruit. You cannot separate fruit from the miraculous. Let me explain. The minister preaches on love and we finally grasp how important love is. We might say, "Love, it's a wonderful idea, Pastor, I'm inspired. By the time we meet next Sunday I'm resolved that through the strength of my own will and sheer determination I'm going to be full of Christian love". It is never that simple!

What is more likely to happen is that over the next few years the Lord will so order things so that he bring into your life people who are hard to love and hard to forgive. The pain that that involves is not something to take on lightly. Then with God's Spirit working upon your will and your spirit, you will start to become loving in the Christian sense if you are prepared to let the Spirit mould you. In the very ordinariness of the situation we can fail to see that this was all Christ's doing through his Spirit. There is a very real aspect of the miraculous in this.

The gifts God in Rom 12:6-8		
1	Prophesying	Gift of the Spirit
2	Serving	Fruit of the Spirit?
3	Teaching	Gift of the Spirit
4	Encouraging	Fruit of the Spirit?
5	Giving	Gift of the Spirit
6	Leadership	Gift of the Spirit
7	Showing mercy	Fruit of the Spirit

What do you say, especially if you are not as young as you used to be? Some might be tempted to think, "Ted, I'm just too set in my ways to worry about God's gifts". For my remaining years I'm content to work on the fruit, (cramming for my finals as an old friend put it) but you have encouraged me to ask the Spirit for help". Well it is never as simple as that either. Take Romans 12: 6-13. Paul talks about believers practicing the gifts God has given them. But look what he now calls gifts. He starts with what you would expect, prophesying, and teaching and then he throw in things that look more like fruit, serving, mercy and then launches straight into love, not as a more excellent way but the natural companion of God's gifts. After we have made such hard and fast categories of gifts and fruit, Paul goes and stirs them all up and calls them gifts, but not of the Spirit, rather of God.

Isn't this really quite simple? What have we ever received from our Father in heaven that was not ultimately his gift, every breath we take, the rain in its season, the sun by day and the moon by night, our health, our prosperity. But are you thinking, "Ted, there is nothing special about this, it is all very ordinary. It rains on my neighbour and he is a sinner, how am I better off"?

You are better off because God sent the greatest gift, his own dearly beloved Son who died for you just as he died for your neighbour - but he has given you the gift of faith. It is only through that gift that you can see the beauty of his dear son. As for your neighbour, if I may paraphrase Acts 18:17, "God's gifts are poured out on him also so that he may seek Him and perhaps reach out for Him and find Him, though He is not far from each one of us. We are blessed to know the gift of that closeness".

So, has a lapsed Pentecostal lost his interest in gifts and wants us to return to the old ways? Let me tell you why that could never be. Back in 1988, Rachel, my lovely wife, was diagnosed with aggressive breast cancer. She had initially gone to hospital for a routine removal of a lump. I was not expecting the doctor to come out to talk with me about whether it was even worth treating because of how far it had progressed. I had been told Rachel was not in the right age group and the lump was not in the place you would expect for cancer. It was all just routine. Before this time, I had arrogantly thought my faith was so strong that nothing could shake it. My path of faith had been difficult to that point and each trial seemed to strengthen it. Yet, in a moment it was cut down. And just then I thought I heard a little inner voice – "you have received so many good things from God's hands and now is the time to pay for them – as the scriptures say "To whom much is given much is required". As I went back to the room to wait for Rachel to be wheeled back from recovery, I realised that across the hall a couple of months earlier, my aunt had been diagnosed with cancer. She had called on the Uniting Church elders. They prayed and she was healed. That voice came again. "Lightning doesn't strike in the same place twice. What are your chances of a miracle? You know they are rare". The coming days were a nightmare as I felt God had deserted me and I couldn't find Him anywhere. In my desperation, one evening I did something so very uncharacteristic of me. I opened my Bible at random and cried out in prayer, "Lord I have to hear from you" and with my eyes closed put my finger on the page. There, under my finger, were the words of Luke 19:26 "I tell you that to everyone who has, more will be given". My wife who was given two years to live is still with me, 24 years later.

It really is as simple as that. We serve a Lord who is the "giver of every good and perfect gift" (James 1:17). It is his nature to give. As to that small voice that said it was time to pay, I used to say it was the enemy of my soul. In hindsight, rather I fear it was my own hard heart that refuses to totally believe that God's gifts were only ever of grace and mercy and that I may somehow have deserved them or that I can in some way pay for them.

While I may be a lapsed Pentecostal, God's gifts are as precious to me as life itself but I can't look at what our family received and say "Look what our spirituality has dragged from the heart of God". Like you, I have seen far better people than Rachel and I travel a far different route through their suffering. Spiritual encounters and spirituality are two entirely different things. Gifts are neither a sign of possession by the evil one or of exceptional divine approval. Spirituality is the true gift. Paul urged the Corinthian believers to seek the better gifts (1 Cor. 12:31). I have heard this said that the better gifts are prophecy and the healing. After encountering people speak boldly in God's name when He was silent, and "healers" that use whatever gifts they have for financial gain I now question that. A life well lived now seems to me to be the greatest gift.

May we never cease to give thanks to our loving Saviour whose nature it is to give, even to the undeserving. May we never be hesitant or fearful to approach him with our every need for he is more ready to hear and answer than we know. Mat 10 [29] "Aren't two sparrows sold for a penny? Yet not one of them will fall to the ground apart from the will of your father. [30]and even the very hairs of your head are all numbered. [31]so don't be afraid; you are worth more than many sparrows".

10. GRACE MERCY AND PEACE

Setting: *Pastor Ian was going to start a series of sermons from First and Second Timothy and Titus dealing with the topic of handing on the baton of leadership. He had asked me to preach on the introduction to First Timothy, setting the scene for his sermons that follow.*

Reading: Acts 20:13-37 – Paul's farewell to the Ephesian Elders

Text: 1 Timothy 1:1-11

1 Paul, an apostle of Christ Jesus by the command of God our Savior and of Christ Jesus our hope,

2 To Timothy my true son in the faith:

Grace, mercy and peace from God the Father and Christ Jesus our Lord.

3 As I urged you when I went into Macedonia, stay there in Ephesus so that you may command certain people not to teach false doctrines any longer 4 or to devote themselves to myths and endless genealogies. Such things promote controversial speculations rather than advancing God's work—which is by faith. 5 The goal of this command is love, which comes from a pure heart and a good conscience and a sincere faith. 6 Some have departed from these and have turned to meaningless talk. 7 They want to be teachers of the law, but they do not know what they are talking about or what they so confidently affirm.

8 We know that the law is good if one uses it properly. 9 We also know that the law is made not for the righteous but for lawbreakers and rebels, the ungodly and sinful, the unholy and irreligious, for

those who kill their fathers or mothers, for murderers, ¹⁰ for the sexually immoral, for those practicing homosexuality, for slave traders and liars and perjurers—and for whatever else is contrary to the sound doctrine ¹¹ that conforms to the gospel concerning the glory of the blessed God, which he entrusted to me.

Wonder Woman you ask? Ephesus was the city of the Amazons and I told Brett I would open with that image, but being a true courageous preacher of the word I decided that discretion was the better part of valour and I am now leaving the subject of women's ministry to Pastor Ian.

The books of First and Second Timothy were written by the aged Paul to his most trusted deputy, his true son in the faith. Things were going so wrong in the Ephesian church that only the best man available must be sent. He was, in a sense, the first Intentional Interim Pastor.

The Pastoral Epistles, in part, talk to me about the certainty and uncertainty that stand side by side in our Christian faith. Have you experienced the uncertainty that can be associated with our faith? Have you prayed about something, and sought the Lord's guidance, have you been sure of his clear direction for the way forward. Have you ever then had that certainty dashed on the hard reality of events as they unfold? If so, you are in very good company.

What about the uncertainty of our Christian faith? Paul spent three years establishing the church in Ephesus, the capital of the province of Asia. It was a Greek city despite being in modern day Turkey; it was also a very rich city and the centre of the worship of Artemis. The population were devoted to her worship. Her Temple is described as the greatest of the seven wonders of the ancient world. Yet despite this, Paul established a church so vibrant that his critics said (Acts 19:26) "you see and hear how this fellow Paul has convinced and led astray large numbers of people here in Ephesus and in practically the whole province of Asia." Things eventually got too hot for Paul in the city after the riot we read of in Acts 19 so he went off to Greece. Only months later, he was back in the region where he met with the Ephesian elders in a nearby town.

The elders were heartbroken when Paul said "Now I know that none of you among whom I have gone about preaching the kingdom will ever see me again". He was driven by the Spirit and yet here is Paul back again and planning another visit (1 Tim 3:14). Have you ever heard God's whisper? I have and I am sure you have too. To my shame I have only ever led two people to Christ, both of them on their way to commit suicide. Both times there was a very real sense of urgency to talk to them, it was probably more than a whisper but easy to shrug off none the less. But our Christian life is very far from praying down a predetermined script for our life that we can follow without detours and dry gullies, without mishearing. I wanted to be a pilot with MAF, then I wanted to be a missionary and then I wanted to be a pastor. None of these things I had the gifts for or the health yet I felt a very strong urge, and dare I say calling, within me. I ended up being a sawmiller instead. What of you and your career and relationship and the myriad of decisions that impact on your life?

But there is more to say about uncertainty from Paul's charge to the Ephesian Elders. He said [29] "I know that after I leave, savage wolves will come in among you and will not spare the flock. [30] Even from your own number men will arise and distort the truth in order to draw away disciples after them." Consider again the uncertainty. Paul, the great apostle, the great inspired writer whose words men ponder over for the slightest shade of meaning, who could raise the dead, whose sweatbands could raise the sick, whose ministry could see many renounce the magic spells of Artemis, who had reliable insights into the future, made mistakes when it came to choosing his elders. And the church has been faced with the same issue over the millennia, imperfect people who hear imperfectly have to choose imperfect people who will lead them imperfectly. And yes, it can go wrong.

In the book of Acts we see Paul appointing his elders after a very short time, perhaps in only a matter of months. He had no other option initially and it seemed to work but now the undesirability of this hasty practice has come home to roost. Timothy will be given very clear directions about who is to be appointed as leaders in the church in the future. The criteria will not be who can say "Thus says the Lord" the loudest and more often, or could say with certainty, "God said to me this morning". He set before Timothy a yard stick by which to measure men and women and it is all character. You see the elders who would become heretics and savage wolves in the midst of the church probably did all this, but the one thing they lacked was character.

Many books have been written on what the actual heresy was. I only give 27 pages to it in my *Introduction to the Pastoral Epistles*. There are a few clues, but it is impossible to pin down, some of what is said is so general that it applies to all generations. Paul doesn't even bother to refute it, after all how do you refute myths and endless genealogies? The belief was not so much the problem but the practices and here Paul is specific. Paul calls these men for what they are:

- Heretics who taught for financial reward 1 Tim 6:5; Tit 1:11
- They deceived 2 Tim 3:13
- They were hypocrites 2 Tim 3:5; Tit 1:16, 3:8-9
- They argued over words not substance 1 Tim 1:4, 6; 4:2; 2 Tim 2:14, 16, 23; Tit 1:10; 3:9
- There is a list of vices 1 Tim 1:9-10; 2 Tim 3:2-4
- They had success among women (the most venerable) 2 Tim 3:6

But, I said that alongside the uncertainty there was certainty. The heretics wanted to be teachers of the Law, the Law is good they said and Paul agrees - now ladies at this point I would like you to close your eyes and stop your ears.

(Image is of a rabbi's circumcision kit)

If I said to the men, "I have arranged for Dr. Rosenberg[13] to come out this morning with his little kit so we can so we can walk through the door of Judaism so we could be true Christians" it would be a short queue indeed. Unfortunately, the New Testament tells us that many early gentile Christians were lining up to be circumcised.

You can open your eyes now ladies. But our queue would be short,

---

13 A former local Jewish doctor who served us into his 80's. he was very happy to do 8th day circumcisions.

not because we lack the commitment to our faith that they had but because firstly we understand the role of the Law, yes it is good, it shows us what sin is and exposes us as sinners in need of a saviour. But secondly alongside that we understand that there is a saviour, a saviour that forgives our sins and it is completely through grace.

Probably the main reason Paul doesn't argue with the heretics is because, by that time, the truth is a deposit which is taken for granted. His "argument" is simply to remind the Ephesian church of what they already know to be true, of the "sound doctrine that conforms to the gospel concerning the glory of the blessed God,". Paul reminds them of five reliable sayings. These are not just an early creed but the considered and tried opinion which had lodged in the heart of the Christian community. These creeds show Christianity had already found its mould. Christ's mercy and long-suffering is the opposite of Jewish myths and Mosaic genealogies. Patience is a characteristic that must describe the lives and ministry of all Christians.

The Five *Reliable Sayings* of Paul are;

1 Tim. 1:15	Christ Jesus came into the world to save sinners.
1 Tim. 3:1	If anyone sets his heart on being an overseer he desires a noble task.
1 Tim. 4:9-10	We have put our hope in a living God who is saviour to all men.
2 Tim. 2:11-13	If we died with Him we will also live with Him. If we endure we will also reign with Him. If we disown Him He will also disown us. If we are faithless He will remain faithful for He cannot disown himself.
Titus 3:4-8	When the kindness and love of God our Saviour appeared He saved us. Not because of righteous things we have done but because of His mercy. He

> saved us through the washing of rebirth and renewal by the Holy Spirit, Whom He poured out on us generously through Jesus Christ our saviour, so that having been justified by grace we might become heirs with the hope of eternal life.

We might think God has spoken to us and find he has not. We might think the Lord is in a certain action and events prove otherwise. What we thought was the Lord might just have been a dodgy curry from the local Indian. But these five saying remain the rock on which nothing can shake us.

How do we, and how do the pastors, elders, deacons and everyone else who is involved in the ministry of this church, and that is most of us, live with the tension of uncertainty and certainty? Of our failures mixed in with our successes? Even if you aren't involved any longer in ministry the question still applies to you. There is good advice in Paul's greeting to Timothy. He wants his son to receive "Grace, mercy and peace from God the Father and Christ Jesus our Lord". The ordinary word for greeting in a Greek letter was *chairein* – rejoice, but Paul uses *charis* or as we know it, grace, a word play that turns a greeting into a desire for blessing from God, a blessing that was unearned and undeserved. In a single word he expresses the faithful saying, "Christ Jesus came into the world to save sinners." He also wishes "peace" upon Timothy; To this day it is the greeting of the Jews, *shalom*. Peace in this troubled world is the gift promised by our Lord in John 14:27 "Peace I leave with you; my peace I give you. I do not give to you as the world gives. Do not let your hearts be troubled and do not be afraid." Timothy could have peace in mind and heart because he had first of all found peace with God.

Grace and peace, this is the usual greeting in all Paul's letters but for Timothy he asks grace, mercy and peace. There is an extra blessing that Paul asks for his true son, mercy. I have spoken a couple of times of that Hebrew concept of *hesed*, perhaps best translated with the word loving-kindness. The Greek Old Testament of the time called the Septuagint used the same word for loving-kindness as Paul uses here. Consider Timothy's nature

- His natural timidity, 1 Cor 16:10&11; 2 Tim 1:7
- His youth, 1 Tim 4:12; 2 Tim 2:22
- Frequent ailments, 1 Tim 5:23. This would not encourage travel which was perilous at best.
- Being a little negligent, needing to stir up the gifts in him, 1 Tim 4:12-16; 2 Tim 1:6, 3:14ff

Such an imperfect man was set aside as a leader, and a leader who had to deal with some serious strife. Strife indeed that might seem beyond a man of his disposition. Well I am no longer young but there was a time when all four applied to me, what of you? When faced with the uncertainty and certainty of our faith we all need that extra blessing of loving-kindness. There are times when we have to remember, as Timothy was reminded, that our relationship with our heavenly father is not like that of others. To quote one commentator "Because the Biblical concept of mercy was governed by that of covenant, the concept of mercy developed the connotation of help or kindness that could be asked or requested of a superior, but never demanded". Timothy is reminded of a gracious saviour, he is reminded of the peace that comes from being reconciled to the father and he is reminded of his right to go before him and ask for help. We all at times need to be reminded of that.

What better closing prayer can I leave with you than Paul's words to Timothy. May you all experience grace, mercy and peace from God the Father and Christ Jesus our Lord

11. WALK WITH GOD

Stephen Beasley, our very reliable church treasurer and his wife Robyn have been a very close friends for over thirty years. Stephen was a lecturer in farm management at the University of Queensland.

Bible Reading: Gen 5: 3-32

Introduction - Long marches

On one of my trips to East New Britain in PNG, my mate and I and a couple of staff from the University went for a walk "trek" up into the Baining Mountains. We drove to the end of the road and then walked up and down and across a couple of river fords. Eventually I got to the point where I stopped. At times my foot was wider than the footpath and I knew that if I went any further I would have real difficulty getting home. My mate and the guide went about another kilometer and reached the village. My mate was the 2nd white man to have been to the village – the other was the German priest.

This experience gave me a new respect for the diggers who fought on the Kokoda Track. The Kokoda Trail or Track is a single-file foot thoroughfare that runs 96 kilometres (60 miles) overland — 60 kilometres (37 miles) in a straight line — through the Owen Stanley Range in Papua New Guinea. The track is the most famous in Papua New Guinea and is renowned as the location of the World War II battle between Japanese and Australian forces in 1942.

The track starts, or ends, at Owens Corner in Central Province, 50 kilometres (31 miles) east of Port Moresby, and then crosses rugged and isolated terrain, which is only passable on foot, to the village of Kokoda in Oro Province. It reaches a height of 2,190 metres (7,185 ft) as it passes around the peak of Mount Bellamy.

Hot, humid days with intensely cold nights, torrential rainfall and the risk of endemic tropical diseases such as malaria make it a challenge to walk.

The Long March

The Long March (October 1934 – October 1935) was an historic journey of 6,000 miles, in which Communist army forces fled their bases in Jiangxi province in south China. Surrounded by the Nationalist army of Chiang Kai-shek, some 80,000 soldiers of the Red Army escaped and headed north. Only 8,000 to 9,000 survived the trek, which ended in the establishment of a new Communist base in Yan'an. The Long March became the central event in Chinese revolutionary mythology

There were other forced Marches – in WW2 as the Allies closed in on the Germans, a large number of prisoners were forced to march in atrocious conditions away from Prison Camps.

"The March" refers to a series of death marches during the final stages of the Second World War in Europe. From a total of 257,000 western Allied prisoners of war held in German military prison camps, over 80,000 POWs were forced to march westward across Poland, Czechoslovakia, and Germany in extreme winter conditions, over about four months between January and April 1945. This series of events has been called various names: "The Great March West", "The Long March", "The Long Walk", "The Long Trek", "The Black March", "The Bread March", but most survivors just called it "The March".

All of these walks pale into insignificance when we look at the walk of Enoch. In Genesis 5 we have a shortened report of the time between Adam and Noah. Adam the first man and Noah the man who would start a new history and a new family after the flood.

The reading is like going to the cemetery where we see the tombstones – here lies so-and-so: Born Died. Here it is Born, had children after so many years, lived so many more and died.

Except for Enoch – Enoch has the record for the longest walk. I love the story told of an aboriginal girl who paraphrased the end of Enoch's walk with God as "God said to Enoch, we have walked so far that you'd better come home with me – it's too far to go back!"

12. FORGIVENESS

Reading: Psalm 18:20-26

To the choirmaster. A Psalm of David, the servant of the LORD, who addressed the words of this song to the LORD on the day when the LORD rescued him from the hand of all his enemies, and from the hand of Saul. He said:

²⁰ The LORD dealt with me according to my righteousness; according to the cleanness of my hands he rewarded me.
²¹ For I have kept the ways of the LORD, and have not wickedly departed from my God.
²² For all his rules were before me, and his statutes I did not put away from me.
²³ I was blameless before him, and I kept myself from my guilt.
²⁴ So the LORD has rewarded me according to my righteousness, according to the cleanness of my hands in his sight.
²⁵ With the merciful you show yourself merciful; with the blameless man you show yourself blameless;
26 with the purified you show yourself pure; and with the crooked you make yourself seem tortuous.

John 8:2-11

Text: John 8 2-11

² At dawn he appeared again in the temple courts, where all the people gathered round him, and he sat down to teach them. ³ The teachers of the law and the Pharisees brought in a woman caught in adultery. They made her stand before the group⁴ and said to Jesus, 'Teacher, this woman was caught in the act of adultery. ⁵ In the Law Moses commanded us to stone such women. Now what do you say?' ⁶ They were using this question as a trap, in order to have a basis for accusing him.

But Jesus bent down and started to write on the ground with his finger. ⁷ When they kept on questioning him, he straightened up and said to them, 'Let any one of you who is without sin be the first to throw a stone at her.' ⁸ Again he stooped down and wrote on the ground.

⁹ At this, those who heard began to go away one at a time, the older ones first, until only Jesus was left, with the woman still standing there. ¹⁰ Jesus straightened up and asked her, 'Woman, where are they? Has no one condemned you?'

¹¹ 'No one, sir,' she said.

'Then neither do I condemn you,' Jesus declared. 'Go now and leave your life of sin.'

David was finally at ease; Saul no longer sought to kill him as he was slain by his enemies. David's enemies around were subdued and he was king over all Israel. He could finally sleep with both eyes closed. In gratitude he penned a psalm of praise where he reflected on God's goodness to him. In that psalm where he praises that goodness, David reminds the father of his goodness to him - ²³ I was blameless before him, and I kept myself from my guilt. ²⁴ So the LORD has rewarded me according to my righteousness, according to the cleanness of my hands in his sight. He was still a relatively young man, perhaps in his early thirties, with more than half his life ahead of him and he had laid down the path he expected the rest of his life to follow.

And then in his ease, David finally felt secure enough to let the annual business of war to his generals and he stayed at home. One day he went to the roof of his palace and looked out and saw Bathsheba bathing. She was the wife of Uriah the Hittite, one of his most trusted and loyal soldiers. Desire awakened in this King who had many wives and he sent for her. She became pregnant and when it became obvious that his sin would be exposed he had Uriah murdered and stole his wife. He had forgotten his own words ²⁶ "with the purified you show yourself pure; and with the crooked you make yourself seem tortuous."

David, who had earlier been so pleased with his own righteousness shrugged off the news of the murder (2 Sam 11:25) "Don't let this upset you; the sword devours one as well as another. Press the attack against the city and destroy it.' Say this to encourage Joab." The war went well and life continued as normal and David didn't know how deeply he had displeased the one who is the true judge of righteousness. He didn't know how quickly he had gone from being blameless by God's laws to despising those very same precepts.

It took a parable from a courageous prophet for David to understand his sin and that by his own judgement was not fit to live. To understand that the high and mighty are no more before the Lord than the lowest of the low. But it wasn't simply a matter of going to the confessional and receiving absolution from a priest. In a moment the whole weight of the law came down upon him for its penalty was clear and in it there was no forgiveness for sins like this. The depths of his struggle to find forgiveness are found in the seven penitential Psalms, Psalm 6, 32, 38, 51, 102, 130 and 142 In these psalms we see the agony of the conviction of his sin in words like "I am worn out from my groaning. All night long I flood my bed with weeping and drench my couch with tears. And "For day and night your hand was heavy on me; my strength was sapped as in the heat of summer."

Yet in his struggle he started to see a flicker of light, that God could forgive him, that God might forgive him and, finally, that God had forgiven him. After the battle he declared, Psm. 130 [3]"If you, Lord, kept a record of sins, Lord, who could stand? [4] But with you there is forgiveness, so that we can, with reverence, serve you."

When we learnt the history of our young nation we should have had respect of our early explorers who endured great hardship to traverse our land on foot or horseback without a map to guide them. But where they struggled and sometimes perished, we now travel in speed and comfort along a well signposted road. Likewise David explored the path of conviction and sorrow for sin and discovered a loving and forgiving saviour. Really, you do not see much about repentance before David's fall, certainly not with the patriarchs or Moses. David started his path of discovery reminding God of his own faithfulness but ends in his penitential psalms reminding himself of God's faithfulness – Psm. 32:10 " but the Lord's unfailing love (Hesed) surrounds the one who trusts in him". Now the route to forgiveness is clearly marked and there is no excuse for us to make hard weather on the path to restoration and friendship with our maker.

Who of us would dare to say before God, "I was blameless before him, and I kept myself from my guilt. So the LORD has rewarded me according to my righteousness?" There is not one of us who has not stumbled, true not all of us here have been adulterers or murderers but "If we claim to be without sin, we deceive ourselves and the truth is not in us," (1 John 1:8). There is not one of us in this chapel, or this valley, or this nation that can say we have not offended our maker in word, thought or deed. My sole purpose today is to remind you what you already know and to point you again, not one who is our judge and accuser but a loving saviour who came into the world to save sinners (1 Tim 1:15) and to bring us to God (1 Peter 3:18). These are familiar paths to you, and for many they were trod by your parents and their parents before them. It would be the earnest desire of us all that they will be paths our children will tread as well.

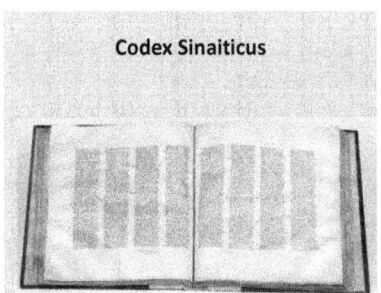

But this gospel of a forgiving saviour was not always preached and not always welcomed by the church. Imagine, if you can, that you are a pastor in the early church about 1800 years ago. A young man comes to you in deep distress for soul, why, because like David before him, he has committed adultery. He wants to know, can he find forgiveness, or will he forever live in the torment of Hell. Is his saviour able to be a saviour?

Well, as a good pastor you go to your Bible and it happens to be an early copy of what we know as the Codex Sinaiticus (4th century), one of the most important hand-written ancient copies of the Greek Bible. You look it up and you have some bad news for him. Jesus never forgave a baptised believer of adultery. You see, the passage of the woman caught in adultery, my text this morning, is missing as it is in many translations now. So you look further and see in Hebrews 10:26 "For if we wilfully persist in sin (wilfully sin NKJV) after having received the knowledge of the truth, there no longer remains a sacrifice for sins, [27] but a fearful prospect of judgment, and a fury of fire that will consume the adversaries".

Now this passage is probably meant to refer to "a certain [un-repairable] form of apostasy, adopted as a settled policy by [some] one who had once accepted Christianity and later, [just] as deliberately, decided to renounce it." Unfortunately it does not say that and many in the early church took it straight at face value. "Young man, the scriptures offer you no hope, get used to the heat because it is hot where you are going." But then he remembers, this old Bible has at the back a book called the *Shepherd of Hermas*. The Shepherd of Hermes is a work of the second century that had such great authority that leading early church fathers considered it as scripture. This authority is why it is found in with the Codex Sinaiticus. He asks the young man, "How many times have you committed adultery"? "Twice." is the reply. Then he gives him the news," Son you are certainly going to burn."

The Shepherd of Hermas, the young only man's hope of escape, taught that there was forgiveness for sin after baptism but God's grace could cover only one sin and not a second. Tertullian one of the leading church fathers thought that this was very lax and called Hermas, the Shepherd of the Adulterers.

They had been interpreting the scriptures without sanctified reason and very soon had to start categorising sins into their seriousness to offer some hope. This is where the idea of "deadly sins" came from. It came to a head in Rome under Callistus, Bishop of Rome from 217 to 222. He ruled "that sincere penitents might be readmitted to Christian communion even after adultery and fornication." This was considered criminal laxity and for a time the church in Rome split under a second bishop. John Chrysostom (c 347–407), the golden mouthed preacher, allowed for forgiveness of two or even three serious sins. Going to a doctor for a second opinion I can understand, but going to a second theologian for an opinion on your adultery is just plain ridiculous.

I fear that many of these men would have been queuing up with their stones, "Me first, for I am without sin." Sadly today many churches are not places of healing, "preferring fresh blood to spilt blood" as one writer said.

Some advice for sinners

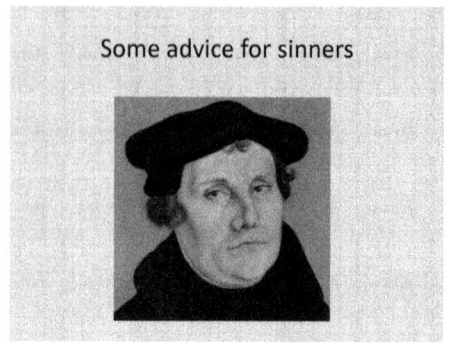

So, I ask you, do we have a saviour who is no saviour at all and wishes only to condemn you through setting the bar impossibly high. Or do we have a saviour who is the friend of sinners. So what advice can I give you? You have known the scriptures since Sunday school and you only need to meditate on them. What comes to mind is the advice given by Martin Luther to his friend Philip Melanchthon and that was on one hand to "Sin boldly". Of course it is hyperbolae but his point was to own what we are and not be like the Pharisee who thanked God that he was not like other men, and only needed a little bit of salvation. Don't be ashamed to say you are a sinner and need a saviour. On the other hand he told his friend to believe and rejoice in Christ more boldly.

In an imaginary conversation with the devil, the accuser of his soul, Luther wrote "by calling me a sinner you are supplying me with weapons against yourself so that I can slay and destroy you with your own sword; for Christ died for sinners. Furthermore, you yourself proclaim the glory of God to me; you remind me of God's paternal love for me, a miserable and lost sinner; for He so loved the world that He gave His Son (John 3:16). Again, whenever you throw up to me that I am a sinner, you revive in my memory the blessing of Christ, my Redeemer, on whose shoulders, and not on mine, lie all my sins; for "the Lord hath laid on Him the iniquity of us all" and "for the transgression of His people was He stricken" (Is. 53:6-8). Therefore when you throw up to me that I am a sinner, you are not terrifying me; you are comforting me beyond measure."

Am I saying we should live a life of deep introspection and remorse? There is certainly a time for it, and for many of us it was when Christ was drawing us to himself, before we had looked to the cross and seen our fathers love and acceptance. That very love causes us to keep a very short account and give us the confidence to come boldly before him without fear or condemnation.

We find David repeating our Psalm in 2 Samuel 22 shortly before his death. He had learnt that his greatest enemies quite probably were inward with backsliding and his own sinful passions. Yet, with an innocent man's blood on his hands he repeats the same words we heard Greg read earlier that his hands were clean. We are as all people most foolish if we do not leave here with clean hands and a pure heart for our father's promise is that (Psm. 103:12) "as far as the east is from the west, so far has he removed our transgressions from us."

John 8:2-11

In the wonderful story of the woman caught in adultery, when confronted with their own sinfulness, the religious leaders who thought they were so righteous slunk away one by one. Only one remained to hear the words, "I do not condemn you", the woman caught in the very act. May we never slink away from our saviour but be blessed to hear those words from our saviour and go and sin no more.

13. INTRODUCTION TO DANIEL

Pastor Ian was to deliver a series on the book of Daniel and I was asked to give an introduction to the series.

Reading: 2 Kings 24:1-7

During Jehoiakim's reign, Nebuchadnezzar king of Babylon invaded the land, and Jehoiakim became his vassal for three years. But then he turned against Nebuchadnezzar and rebelled. ² The LORD sent Babylonian, Aramean, Moabite and Ammonite raiders against him to destroy Judah, in accordance with the word of the LORD proclaimed by his servants the prophets. ³ Surely these things happened to Judah according to the LORD's command, in order to remove them from his presence because of the sins of Manasseh and all he had done, ⁴ including the shedding of innocent blood. For he had filled Jerusalem with innocent blood, and the LORD was not willing to forgive.

⁵ As for the other events of Jehoiakim's reign, and all he did, are they not written in the book of the annals of the kings of Judah? ⁶ Jehoiakim rested with his ancestors. And Jehoiachin his son succeeded him as king.

⁷ The king of Egypt did not march out from his own country again, because the king of Babylon had taken all his territory, from the Wadi of Egypt to the River Euphrates.

Text: 2 Sam 7:11-16

"'The LORD declares to you that the LORD himself will establish a house for you:¹² When your days are over and you rest with your ancestors, I will raise up your offspring to succeed you, your own flesh and blood, and I will establish his kingdom. ¹³ He is the one

who will build a house for my Name, and I will establish the throne of his kingdom forever. ¹⁴ I will be his father, and he will be my son. When he does wrong, I will punish him with a rod wielded by men, with floggings inflicted by human hands. ¹⁵ But my love will never be taken away from him, as I took it away from Saul, whom I removed from before you. ¹⁶ Your house and your kingdom will endure forever before me; your throne will be established forever.'"

Introduction

Pastor Iain plans to deliver a series of sermons on the book of Daniel. Perhaps he is going to unwrap the mysteries of this book that foretell the history of the world up to our Lord's return. I suspect not. His messages will concentrate on how we might live as believers in an unbelieving world. So I don't plan to steal his thunder so as to speak. He has set for me the task of delivering an introduction to this book.

When Gods people are unfaithful to God

It is a good choice of a book to study. It starts with a king who failed to plead before God to cleanse the land of its sin. Stan's reading shows the sins of Manessah are directly linked to the setting of Daniel and gives us the historical setting of the book. Paul says of the Greek pagans in Acts 17 30 *"In the past God overlooked such ignorance, but now he commands all people everywhere to repent. 31 For he has set a day when he will judge the world with justice by the man he has appointed. He has given proof of this to everyone by raising him from the dead."* But here there is no winking of God's eye, the kings and the people had done things that were not ignorant, but detestable.

> **detestable practices**
>
> engaging in the detestable practices of the nations the LORD had driven out before the Israelites inolved
> - Killing the innocent children
> - Inappropriate practices in the temple
> - Practicing divination
> - Consulting the dead

Manasseh had set his people an example which they followed when he sacrificed his own son and to crown it all, set up male prostitutes in God's temple. This they agreed is what God needs to keep him happy and gain his favour. Now, we are civilised and educated and enlightened and yet we murder approximately 80,000 innocents per year in our nation alone and we exult in the rise of homosexuality and say "let them marry." While there are some that condone this behaviour from the pulpit, just as the priests of God forsook the God they were called to serve, generally, as a nation we say, "God doesn't care" or more likely, "There is no consequence as God does not exist".

But the message of Daniel is firstly, God does care how a nation lives and there can be a consequence for the individual and the land. Solomon in his wisdom observed what every leader and people should know, Proverbs 14 "^{34} Righteousness exalteth a nation: but sin is a reproach to any people". What will we say when God judges those who did the detestable practices of the heathen when our national guilt is probably greater.

Daniel Stood Between his People and God

There is eventually a price to pay and righteous Daniel learnt that the godly pay it along with the unrighteous. Who will dare to be a Daniel standing before God and confess the sin of this land and seek his mercy? Part of Daniel's prayer in Chapter Nine is *[4]"Lord, the great and awesome God, who keeps his covenant of love with those who love him and keep his commandments, [5] we have sinned and done wrong. We have been wicked and have rebelled; we have turned away from your commands and laws."* Will you join with us each Wednesday or on Sunday before church, will you do it in your own home? Because, if we don't who will.

When the world is unfaithful to God

The Languages of Danial

Hebrew: FromDaniel 1:1 to Daniel 2:4a and Chapters 8 through 12,

Aramaic: From Daniel 2:4a (Nebuchadnezzar's dream) to 7:28 (the end of the interpretation of Daniels dream of the four beasts).

Accessible to any literate, Greek, Babylonian or Jew in Daniel's day and later

While we will hear messages from Iain for the church that gathers faithfully here in this chapel in Tent Hill, there is a message in Daniel to those in our valley and our nation and the whole world, a world which had forgotten its dependence on its maker. You see, Daniel is written in two languages. Hebrew is used in Daniel 1:1 to Daniel 2:4a and then from Chapters 8 through 12, Aramaic is used from Daniel 2:4a (Nebuchadnezzar's dream) to 7:28 the end of the interpretation of Daniel's dream of the four beasts. It was a very intentional thing – look at the structure of the Aramaic.

The Structure of the Aramaic

A. Nebuchadnezzar's vision of four kingdoms
  B. God's delivers his servants from a fiery furnace
    C. God's judgement on the pride of Nebuchadnezzar
    C. God's judgement on the pride of Belshazzar
  B. God delivers his servants from a den of lions
A. Daniel's vision of four kingdoms

A Nebuchadnezzar's vision of four kingdoms
    B God's delivers his servants from a fiery furnace
        C God's judgement upon the pride of Nebuchadnezzar
        C God's judgement upon the pride of Belshazzar
    B God delivers his servant from a den of lions
A Daniel's vision of four kingdoms

The Aramaic language was the common language used in Assyrian, Babylonian and Persian communication. Aramaic in Daniel's day is equivalent to English in our day. Daniel's message was not only to the Jewish people, but to the nations. Daniel 2:4 to 7:28 would be accessible to any literate, Greek, Babylonian or Jew in Daniel's day and later. His words were true to Nebuchadnezzar, and Darius and Alexander and to Caesar as their kingdoms' rise and fall are foretold and they are just as true now to Putin, ISIS and Obama and even our new prime minister and all who look to them as a deliverer. It has been there for the last 2500 years for all to read:

The Lord sets up kingdoms and cast them down
The Lord is the one who delivers his saints
The Lord is the one who judges the pride of this world

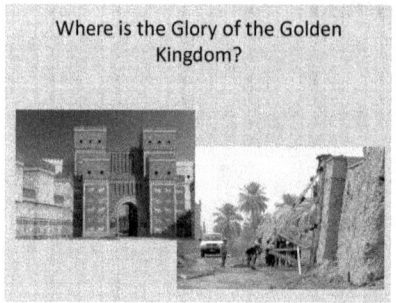

Where is the Glory of the Golden Kingdom?

What must Daniel have thought when he arrived in Babylon, home of two of the seven wonders of the ancient world? Its walls were one of these wonders, where it was said, four chariots could race abreast. Could he have imagined the glory of the whole earth becoming as Jeremiah described it *"Babylon will become a heap of ruins, a haunt of jackals, An object of horror and hissing, without inhabitants"*. Daniel's book paints with broad brushstrokes the kingdoms of this world, present and future and exposes the unseen forces of evil and of good behind the events of history. And it is a history that is not random but working to a timetable. But then it hones in with a single hair brush to look at one man among countless millions. We saw in the beginning of this book Daniel, a godly man, who has lost his inheritance through being caught up in the consequences of the sin of his nation over many generations.

But it ends differently ¹³ "As for you, go your way till the end. You will rest, and then at the end of the days you will rise to receive your allotted inheritance."

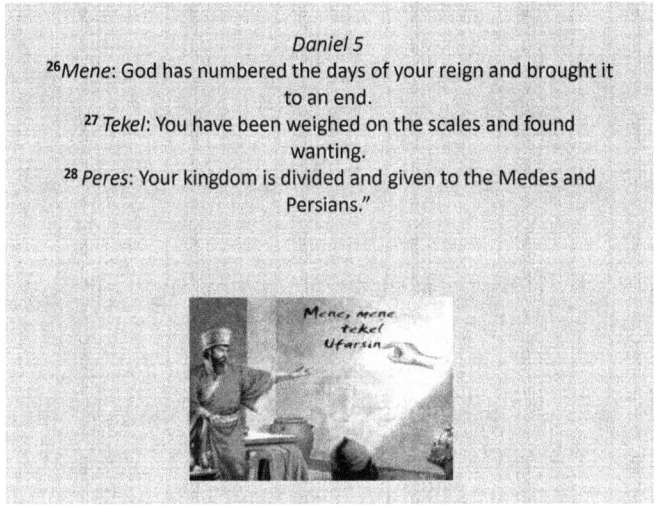

Daniel 5
²⁶*Mene*: God has numbered the days of your reign and brought it to an end.
²⁷ *Tekel*: You have been weighed on the scales and found wanting.
²⁸ *Peres*: Your kingdom is divided and given to the Medes and Persians."

We also, like the empires of old, rise and decline and one day these mortal bodies will be like the dust of Babylon. God has weighed the nations in his balance and found them lacking. One day the stone made without hands of Nebuchadnezzar's dream will strike them and turn their glory to chaff. In that great kingdom that will endure forever, after we have rested, we also will be weighed. We who have put our trust in Christ will never be divided from the one we have trusted. May the Lord give us strength to be faithful to the end when we receive our long awaited inheritance that is worth more than all the kingdoms of this world.

When God appears unfaithful to his people

The Faithful in the Lands of Daniel

So far in my sermon I have been looking at the faithfulness or, more often, lack of faithfulness of men and nations to the saviour but what about God's faithfulness to us? And that brings me to my text. You might have been thinking, "That is a very odd reading for an introduction to Daniel". As we study Daniel's book, it will give us insight into how to live faithful lives in an unfaithful world. But one of the big questions Daniel addresses is, "How should we live when God's promises appear to fail?" And there must be many thousands of Christian families from the lands of Daniel who are pondering a similar question. There the persecution has been cruel and unrelenting and often fatal. And, this is where the covenant to David, hundreds of years before comes in!

God had promised that David's throne was eternal and Yahweh was constantly delivering Judah from the hands of its enemies. But the kings and the people sinned, and sinned badly, so you could, and should, say, "How could God keep on blessing them?" But David's covenant was not like the one at Sinai, "If you will – then I will". It is like God's covenant with you and me – unconditional. *"When he does wrong, I will punish him with a rod wielded by men, with floggings inflicted by human hands. [15] But my love will never be taken away from him, as I took it away from Saul, whom I removed from before you. [16] Your house and your kingdom will endure forever before me; your throne will be established forever."* Have you really grasped grace, the unconditional nature of God's favour on you or are you trying even in some small way trying to earn God's continued faithfulness to you.

Look how God blessed David, conquering all before him, Solomon reigned in peace. But to Daniel and his compatriots it could have looked for all the world as if God's promise of faithfulness has failed and his power was not what they thought. Consider the last kings of Judah.

Manasseh – 697-642 BC	Through to	Zedekiah 597-586 BC
• Did more evil than the nations the LORD had destroyed before the Israelites. • Sacrificed his own son • Deposed and taken captive to Assyria and returned to throne He did evil but repented		• Name changed by Nebuchadnezzar • Jerusalem falls • Sons killed in front of him then blinded • Taken captive to Babylon • Last king of Judah He did evil in the eyes of The Lord

14. Manasseh	697-642 BC	Bad	55	Deposed and Taken captive to Assyria and returned	2 Kings 21:1-18; 2 Chronicles 32:33-33:20
15. Amon	642-640 BC	Bad	2	assassinated	2 Kings 21:18-26; 2 Chronicles 33:20-25
16. Josiah	640-609 BC	Good	31	Renewed the covenant Killed fighting Pharaoh	2 Kings 21:26 – 23:30; 2 Chronicles 33:25-35:27

17. Eliakim /Jehoahaz	609 BC	Bad	3 months	Dethroned by pharaoh	2 Kings 23:30-34; 2 Chronicles 36:1-4
18. Jehoiakim	609-598 BC	Bad	11	Taken bound to Babylon	2 Kings 23:34 – 24:6; 2 Chronicles 36:5-8
19. Jehoiachin	598-597 BC	Bad	3 months	Taken to Babylon with articles from the temple and Daniel	2 Kings 24:6-17 2 Chronicles 36:8-10
20. Mattaniah /Zedekiah	597-586 BC	Bad	11	(name changed to Zedekiah by King Nebuchadnezzar of Babylon probably reflects vassal status) Jerusalem falls, Rebelled – sons killed in front of him and eyes put out	2 Kings 24:17 – 25:30 2 Chronicles 36:10-13; Jeremiah 52:1-3; 37-39; Ezekiel 17:13-16

The times were out of joint and little Judah found herself caught up in the conflict of world empires. There was no time, or the opportunity, to develop the kind of ordered life in which a man may settle into a routine confident God is in his heaven and all is right with the world. The eternal throne of Judah had become the plaything of ungodly rulers. Has your heart ever been broken, have you ever been disillusioned, have you ever been in need and prayed fervently and to find that God's promises seem to come to naught. I know some of you have. Have you ever questioned, why bad things happen to good people? I know some of you have.

Daniel must have thought similar things as he walked from

Jerusalem to Babylon with his king bound beside him. He and his friends didn't have the advantage we have of knowing the love of David's greatest son, eternal and a king, not just of Judah but of the universe. They didn't have the advantage of knowing that in their great trials there would be another standing beside them with the appearance of the son of God. They didn't have the advantage then of visions of the kingdoms of this world being playthings in God's hands.

They didn't have the knowledge then of the son of man who would rule over all things *"In my vision at night I looked, and there before me was one like a son of man, coming with the clouds of heaven. He approached the Ancient of Days and was led into his presence. 14 He was given authority, glory and sovereign power; all nations and peoples of every language worshiped him. His dominion is an everlasting dominion that will not pass away, and his kingdom is one that will never be destroyed."*

They did not know the confusion of the Author of Life horribly crucified; they did not know the joy of the empty tomb. They didn't know it yet, Daniel did know or knew of Jeremiah and his prophesies of the humiliation and ultimate restoration of Judah. In all their confusion, they trusted God's word and worshipped Him and were faithful when all else had forsaken. My friends, it is not always easy to worship but worship we can and worship we must. You do not have to understand only to trust.

Conclusion

Daniel shows us the tension that existed in the lives of the faithful Old Testament saints. On one hand we have the eternal promises of grace as seen in God's selection of David's throne and Zion, sworn with an oath he will not revoke (Psm. 132:11-16) and on the other the need to lead ethical lives based on another covenant, the covenant given to Moses. Israel failed badly and for a time was separated from land and king and temple though their God was never very far from them.

For the world that has rejected grace they have unknowingly accepted to be judged by God's law, a law written on the heart of all men and women, and Daniel's visions promises that that day will come. But for we who glory in grace sometimes need to be reminded that grace does not exist in a vacuum. We may sometimes need to be reminded that grace is made evident to all is a consistent life of faith, a life separated from the abominable practices that can exist around us. May it be said of us, as it was of Daniel, "We will never find any basis for charges against this man Daniel unless it has something to do with the law of his God."

May we also be people who, through all the uncertainties of this life, never cease to worship the true king of this world.

14. THE LORD STILL NEEDS DONKEYS

This following sermon was preached on Palm Sunday by the biggest donkey of them all.

Reading Luke 19:28-44,

The triumphal entry

^{28} *After Jesus had said this, he went on ahead, going up to Jerusalem. ^{29} As he approached Bethpage and Bethany at the hill called the mount of olives, he sent two of his disciples, saying to them, ^{30} "go to the village ahead of you, and as you enter it, you will find a colt tied there, which no one has ever ridden. Untie it and bring it here. ^{31} if anyone asks you, 'why are you untying it?' tell him, 'the lord needs it.'"*

^{32} *Those who were sent ahead went and found it just as he had told them. ^{33} as they were untying the colt, its owners asked them, "why are you untying the colt?" ^{34} They replied, "the Lord needs it."*

^{35} *They brought it to Jesus, threw their cloaks on the colt and put Jesus on it. ^{36} As he went along, people spread their cloaks on the road. ^{37} When he came near the place where the road goes down the mount of olives, the whole crowd of disciples began joyfully to praise god in loud voices for all the miracles they had seen:*

^{38} *"Blessed is the king who comes in the name of the lord!"*

"Peace in heaven and glory in the highest!"

^{39} *Some of the Pharisees in the crowd said to Jesus, "Teacher, rebuke your disciples!" ^{40} "I tell you," he replied, "if they keep quiet, the stones will cry out."*

Text: Zechariah 9:9

> *Rejoice greatly, o daughter of Zion!*
>   *Shout, daughter of Jerusalem!*
> *See, your king comes to you,*
>   *Righteous and having salvation,*
>   *Gentle and riding on a donkey,*
>   *On a colt, the foal of a donkey.*

Introduction

I generally don't give my sermons a title but this one I have as it seemed very apt.

I would like us to use our imagination for a while. Imagine we are sitting in church, imagine it is Palm Sunday. Imagine Barry is standing up the back waiting for someone to arrive. I cannot mention names or there would be no lunch. There, it's not hard at all.

Imagine as Barry looks out, two men in flowing robes, turban and long beards walk into the car park. In fact they look just like the men in our slide. The pair go straight to the Spider, look it up and down and shake their heads and he hears them say "He won't be pleased". Then their eyes light up, as they look over to the creek, yes they have seen Barry's Lexus. Their eyes brighten, and they go straight up to it and start hot wiring it. (After all our heroes in the reading were in effect hot wiring a donkey, they were going to take it without permission). In a gracious way Barry asks them what are they doing? And they reply 'The Lord hath need of it". Well what would you say? If they had done that to the Spider they would be in the back of the paddy wagon and I would be thinking about an old English adage about what you do with horse thieves. But what would you say? Fortunately, Barry is a lot more spiritual than me, and I do not say that lightly, perhaps he might say, "I have been expecting you, it's all cleaned and the tank is full, try and have it back by dark." But I am digressing.

Point 1 - Jesus needs a donkey

Look at setting of our Bible reading - Lazarus has just been raised and Jesus is riding on a wave of popularity. It is the Sunday before

Easter and he is heading to Jerusalem. In Luke 19 29-31 Georgie read for us as he approached Bethpage and Bethany at the hill called the Mount of Olives, he sent two of his disciples, saying to them, [30] "Go to the village ahead of you, and as you enter it, you will find a colt tied there, which no one has ever ridden. Untie it and bring it here. [31] If anyone asks you, 'Why are you untying it?' tell him, 'The Lord needs it.'"

The Lord God of the universe wants, no, needs, a donkey!! This donkey was more than just a nice touch to make the story more interesting; the story of untying the donkey is told to us in the three synoptic gospels (Mat 21:5, Mark 11:3) as well as in John's gospel. This whole episode is full of imagery which shouted to the Jews your promised king is coming. The Lord needs a donkey but we know that God does not need anything. When Solomon dedicated his great temple, he said in 2 Chronicles 6:18 But will God really dwell on earth with men? The heavens, even the highest heavens cannot contain thee, how much less this temple I have built. Why on earth would our loving Saviour, Lord and God need a donkey if he didn't need a temple to be known of men. And Matthew tells us why, Matt 21:4&5 This took place to fulfil what was spoken through the prophet: "Say to the daughter of Zion, see your king comes to you, gentle and riding on a donkey, on a colt, the foal of a donkey."

Matthew is quoting Zechariah 9:9. There are two dates in this prophecy, 2nd and 4th year of Darius, 520 and 518 BC so this prophesy was written a long time ago and a long time even before Jesus, it is a small insignificant passage in a small book in the minor prophets.

It was written when Persian Empire at its peak, yet, it spoke of God's coming kingdom. It was written at a time of mighty and powerful rulers but spoke of a king, righteous & gentle. It was written at a time when sin abounded yet spoke of cleansing as they mourned over the one they have pierced. It was written at a time of great uncertainty yet spoke of rolling back of time, sin and strife. At the heart was a prophecy of a king entering Jerusalem, on a donkey

The great day was dawning but where was the donkey? It was only a small part of the prophesy and who would notice if there was no donkey that day? After all, the important person is here. God the father would notice for he is faithful and true to all his promises whether they be big and small

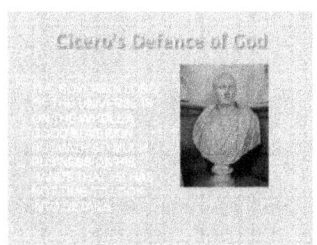

Consider Cicero's apology for Jupiter's neglect of the world, an explanation almost contemporary to our story. The sovereign lord of the universe is on the whole a good sovereign, but with so much business on his hands that he has not time to look into details.

Christians don't know this god, even though at times he looks this way. Our Heavenly Father does look into the details. There was a prophecy to fulfil and he only needed to snap his fingers and a donkey would materialise. He could have repeated the miracle of loaves and fishes. But Jesus said you go and get the donkey. You go and make the prophecy come true. 550 years after Zachariah wrote, there was the donkey tied up just where Jesus said. Not only that, but the heart of the donkey owner was prepared. The disciples were only participating in something that was all of God

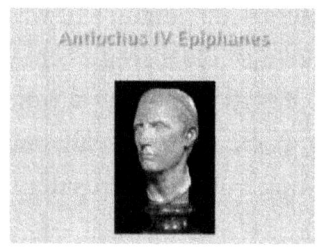

Israel's history over the intervening 550 years following Zachariah were bloody, full of broken dreams, broken bodies and broken hearts. To be honest it looked at best like the god of Cicero where details were not taken care of. Pastor Iain has spoken about the prodigal God who appears careless in his distribution of grace. At times it looked as if he was careless with the lives and welfare of his people. My friends, how have the last couple of years been for you? For some I expect it has brought heartache and frustration, it looks as if God has not taken care of the details. And yet we are all still here this morning to worship him, understanding would be nice but trust is sufficient. We have confidence that despite our present circumstances that all things work together for good and that the donkey will be tied up when and where it needs to be.

That day the Lord needed a donkey and today he still needs donkeys like you and me

Point 2 making the prophecies come true

John was writing perhaps 30 years after the other gospels were written. He had spent a life reflecting on Christ's life. His gospel is very different to the other three. 12:16 at first the disciples did not understand all this. Only after Jesus was glorified did they realize that these things had been written about him and that they had done these things to him. John quotes a scripture in v15:

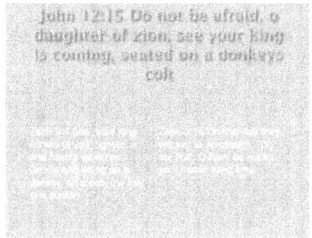

"Do not be afraid, o daughter of Zion, see your king is coming, seated on a donkey's colt."

The problem is, that scripture does not exist! John mixes Zachariah 9:9 in with Zephaniah 3:16. Well what do we say? We could say "The old man was about 90. What else can you expect, he is doing well for his age, I would like to be that good". Or else we could say the beloved apostle had really come to understand what was happening that day

What was going on? These Jews that cheered Jesus knew a few prophecies that they thought were well overdue in fulfilling. If the reluctant prophet was not going to take his role as king we will force him to. The whole story is full of imagery about the king of Israel. Hosanna was the greeting to a king (2 Sam 4:4, 2 Kings 6:26), palm branches were the symbol of nationalism and were used on coins of the second revolt and they quote the messianic psalms. "You disciples think untying the prophesied donkey is big, you've missed the big picture, just you wait till you see Rome trampled underfoot by the Messiah, just wait till you see Jerusalem as the ruler of the world, just you wait till you see the Gentiles subject to the Jews!" This was a triumphant entry worthy of the messianic king who has come to claim his capital and his temple, and we did it, we made it happen.

But the crowd had no idea what this prophecy of a king and a donkey was all about and Jesus said of them Luke 19:42 if you had only known this day what would bring you peace and as a result in John 12:36 he hid himself from them

Point 3 he still needs donkeys

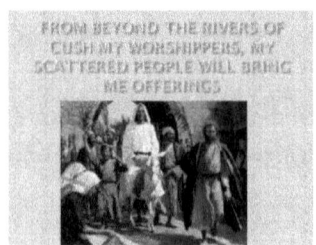

John saw that Jesus was about something totally different. The passage from Zephaniah (the ring in) of his quotation does not speak of a nationalistic king – in 3:9&10 he spoke of people gathered from all over the earth. Then will I purify the lips of the peoples that all of them may call on the name of the Lord and serve him shoulder to shoulder. From beyond the rivers of Cush my worshippers, my scattered people will bring me offerings. It speaks of a king who will rescue the lame and gather those that are scattered 3:19. John remembers different things that were important that day of how the Pharisees said look how the whole world has gone after him (v19). He remembered also what Jesus said when the Greeks sought him – "The hour has now come for the son of man to be glorified" (v20-22). The crowd thought they knew the mind of God better than God himself and thought they could fulfil prophesy. And they would, but not as they thought.

The crowd shouts for him as king of Israel, but the only anointing Jesus receives is an anointing for death. The only crown he will wear is the crown of thorns, the only robe he will wear is the cloak of mockery and when thus anointed and robed he stands before his people and is presented as their king, the crowd will shout, "Crucify him!' In this way they will lift him up to draw all men to him.

The prophesies of grace are there still and unfilled completely. But not one of them has been overlooked even though it may look that way. Christ's command to us is the same as to them - fulfil my prophesies but the Lord has set far more important work for us than untying donkeys. This work is to untie the lost and make his enemies his friends. Soon he will say "Go into all the world and preach the gospel, lo I am with you always."

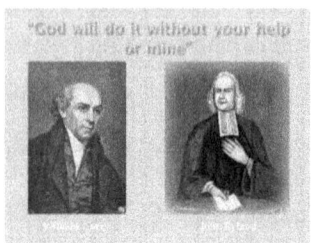

There is a famous dispute in 1786 between John Ryland, the leader of a large number of Baptist churches in England, and William Carey, the great missionary pioneer. After Carey's impassioned plea about the need for missions, Ryland said, "Young man, sit down; when God pleases to convert the heathen, he will do it without your aid and mine." But he won't do it without your help or mine because he has chosen not to do it.

We are not so naive in our thinking as the hyper-calvinists that Ryland represented, who will leave evangelism to the good Lord but perhaps the end result is the same if we are not active in sharing the gospel. Is there an evangelist among us? I have to admit that it is not my gifting - I am only an ordinary businessman or retired businessman these days. But the Easter story is scattered with ordinary people whose lives were sermons;

Mary who anointed Jesus for his burial
The un-names owner of the donkey, or a Lexus
The un-named owner of the upper room
Simon who carried the cross, and
Joseph who buried Jesus when his friends would not.

We don't have to be evangelists but there is a role for us all, Our Lord only asks us to participate in something that was all God.

Let's be perfectly honest, we can all be as stubborn as mules, I remember Edwin Orr, the historian of revival telling the story of an old Presbyterian farmer he heard praying (and it could just as easily be a Baptist), "Lord may I always be right for thou knowest I am hard to turn." Perhaps we need to be turned and actively participate. How? That is between you and God, perhaps to plant, or to water or even to harvest. Or it might be to pray? If I have any ability it has been to enable some men and a remarkable woman in the Philippines and India. Whatever the role given to you, God has promised that he will draw others. "That's a good idea Ted, it can start tomorrow. We will get the minister right on to it when he gets back from holidays". You know the story; the minister is paid to be good etc.

You might say to me that I can't proclaim the gospel, perhaps, but we can all live the gospel. There is great power in a well lived life. Greatness is not found behind the pulpit, but in the living of the gospel. Some years back a Muslim walked into the Lutheran church in Gatton and asked to be baptised. Why? Because Christians did things for him that no Muslim would do for another Muslim. I also remember with great affection Ernie Campbell a council truck driver who showed me how a Christian life could be lived.

If we will let it, the familiar story of Palm Sunday comes to us with a challenge - to actively participate in the fulfilment of great prophesies of grace. Just as we have been untied, he wants us to untie others, to draw all men unto himself.

15. HE CAN BE TRUSTED

This sermon was preached on an Easter Sunday.

Reading: Luke 23:44-49

⁴⁴ It was now about noon, and darkness came over the whole land until three in the afternoon, ⁴⁵ for the sun stopped shining. And the curtain of the temple was torn in two. ⁴⁶ Jesus called out with a loud voice, 'Father, into your hands I commit my spirit.' When he had said this, he breathed his last.

⁴⁷ The centurion, seeing what had happened, praised God and said, 'Surely this was a righteous man.' ⁴⁸ When all the people who had gathered to witness this sight saw what took place, they beat their breasts and went away. ⁴⁹ But all those who knew him, including the women who had followed him from Galilee, stood at a distance, watching these things.

Text: Acts 20:32

³² 'Now I commit you to God and to the word of his grace, which can build you up and give you an inheritance among all those who are sanctified.

Last week I preached at Gatton Baptist Church. I commented on their small lectern and suggested that it probably did not affect the size of the sermon. Today, despite the larger lectern, the message is short. It could be much shorter because of its simplicity but I felt I needed to earn my honorarium which, incidentally, has doubled since the last time. But don't think because it is simple and short it is less important.

Like Tim's choice for Good Friday, our reading and our text are not what you would expect for Easter Sunday. Perhaps a reading about the empty tomb might be more appropriate, but my mind this past week has been on the words of Jesus, "Father, into your hands I commit my spirit." My mind also went to Paul's farewell to the

Ephesian elders, of friends who were parting. And just as Jesus commits his spirit into God's hand, Paul likewise commits his friends into God's hand. This Sunday as well as remembering our risen Lord, we also have come together to commit Rachel's and my long time friends, and indeed friends to many of you, and dear our brother and sister, Steven and Robyn into God's hands as they enter a new phase of their life and ministry. I am also very aware that our dear sister Del has started her treatment and in a different but very real way we must commit her also to God and the word of his grace. Of course there are others and we must not forget our sisters Ula and Joan.

Jesus' words were not his own. A short time before, the full weight of man's sin came upon him and Jesus cried out in despair using the words of David, "My God, my God, why have you forsaken me?" The sun could not shine on the light of the world bearing your sin and mine and he did not address God as father, as he had done earlier, but as the judge of all men. But the sun shone again. Now, David's greatest son again turns to his forefather's hymns and this time calling him "Father", Jesus commits his spirit into his Father's hands. In the psalms these were originally words for the living and, likewise, there is not one of us here that does not need to consciously commit our present and our uncertain future into the hands of the living God.

The uncertainty of cancer treatment for the patient and the anguish that the loved ones know is not a stranger to our family too. In 1988 I took Rachel to Wesley Hospital in Brisbane for the next phase of her cancer treatment. As we approached the hospital she saw the empty cross on the side of the building and she just knew she was in God's hands. Of course, it was an empty cross, the broken body had been taken down and laid in a tomb, the stone rolled across and sealed.

'Tis mystery all: th'Immortal dies:
Who can explore His strange design?
In vain the firstborn seraph tries
To sound the depths of love divine."

And his spirit was placed in the safe keeping of his father's hands and he asks no more of us.

My friends, can our heavenly Father be trusted with what we commit to him? Sadly we live in a generation that increasingly says, "No" and says with equal certainty, "It is not a fearful thing to fall into those hands." The hand that flung stars into space after creating them from nothing are not seen as powerful enough to care for our today let alone our tomorrow. At best the cosmic clockmaker had stood aside from his masterpiece leaving each living creature to fend for itself. The curtain between the creator and his creation was as impenetrable as that which separated the Holy of Holies from the people. At worst, it is all random chaos with our destiny determined by cruel chance.

But the followers of the newly risen Saviour were not such men. They saw that Jesus' Father can be entrusted with that which is committed to him when, three days later, just as Jesus had said, that broken body was restored and glorified and his spirit returned, never to part again. They saw that the verdict of ungodly men was overturned and all the power of this world's governments could not stop God's redeeming plan for this world or for his children. They saw that the worst the evil one could do would not prevent our loving fathers redeeming love rescuing sinners. They knew what Jesus had said about the Father's care for this world, [25] 'Therefore I tell you, do not worry about your life, what you will eat or drink; or about your body, what you will wear. Is not life more than food, and the body more than clothes? [26] Look at the birds of the air; they do not sow or reap or store away in barns, and yet your heavenly

Father feeds them. Are you not much more valuable than they? [27] And he did all this for those of incapable of faith. For those of little faith like you and I, he says, don't worry, your father knows what you need, but seek first the kingdom of God and all this will be added to you. (Matt 6 30-33 paraphrase).

No longer were these just words. They had seen that what was passed from one world to the other was grabbed securely with the loving care of both our father's hands. The children of Israel knew of God's mighty hand, almost always in the singular, a hand that bought judgement and deliverance. There are many references to that hand in the Old Testament, but this is not a hand that holds a cup of judgement but the pair of tender loving hands of a father that that takes the extra care lest anything slip through them.

My friends, we hear a lot these days about fluid or porous borders and how that is causing big problems with men of ill will who exploit them. For you and I also, the border between this kingdom and the kingdom of our Lord is very fluid. But our documentation is in order, immigration and customs know our name for it was sent on ahead and entrusted to our king who wrote it in a very big book kept secure in those two hands that kept Jesus' spirit secure and safe. So, to return to that question, can our Heavenly Father be trusted with what we entrust to him? The new church, empowered by the example and love of Christ and the power of the Spirit resoundingly said "Yes".

In Jesus they found an example for life and, when necessary, an example for death. In the account of the martyrdom of Stephen we read Acts 7 [59] While they were stoning him, Stephen prayed, 'Lord Jesus, receive my spirit.' [60] Then he fell on his knees and cried out, 'Lord, do not hold this sin against them.' When he had said this, he fell asleep." As far as young Saul was concerned, the crime that would seal Stephen's fate was to see the pierced hands of Jesus as he stood at the father's right hand and to commit his own spirit into those loving hands. But for Stephen, his fate was sealed when his name was written in the book in heaven.

Life would take an unexpected turn for Saul, the apostle of the Law, would be overtaken by God's grace on the road to Damascus and he would be set aside to become the apostle to the Gentiles. Saying goodbye to friends he spent years preparing for ministry he says [32] "Now I commit you to God and to the word of his grace, which can build you up and give you an inheritance among all those who are sanctified." Though you may lose a pastor, though you may be separated from the counsel and fellowship of a friend, you will never be separated from the hands of our father into which we commit our lives. These men were elders of the Ephesian church, taught by Paul himself and now, with Paul gone, they were at the top of the tree so as to speak and people would be looking at them as leaders. They, like the church were bought with the blood of Christ and had received the gospel of grace, and now were to preach it.

Paul doesn't pray for safety for them, or provision, but that they may know spiritual blessing, in essence, seeking first the kingdom of God. Most of us have been walking with our saviour for many years and the work of sanctification has been deep. Many of us are gifted in what we have been called to do in the church and we could be tempted to say, "I am all but done, a little bit of polishing of a few rough edges is all that's necessary" But that is not Paul's message. There is still need for the word of his grace to build you up and give you an inheritance. To quote Matthew Henry on the expression, the word of his grace, "Though you are already furnished with good gifts, yet this is able to build you up; there is that in it with which you need to be better acquainted and more affected."

The one direction of the prayer was across the earth-heaven divide to commit his friends into the Father's hands. The other direction of the prayer was from heaven to earth, for the very means of keeping those lives secure. Word and Grace. There is that part of God's message which is the same to all men, to repent, to have faith towards God and trust him with that has been committed to him. "I have known the scriptures from youth," you may say to me. But we lapsed Congregationalists know the truth of their old maxim, "There is yet more light and truth to break forth from his word". We have only paddled around its shore. And of grace, it is unique to every one of us and amazing none the less in its diversity - extraordinary in its power to lead and keep and transform.

There will be that final commitment for those who are being built up by word and grace, and with it the promise of an inheritance. John 14 [1]'Do not let your hearts be troubled. You believe in God; believe also in me. [2] My Father's house has many rooms; if that were not so, would I have told you that I am going there to prepare a place for you? [3] And if I go and prepare a place for you, I will come back and take you to be with me that you also may be where I am. [4] You know the way to the place where I am going.' There will be no bad surprises on the other side, otherwise he would have told us and we will be absent from him no longer.

Conclusion

Let me quote another commentator. "Those hands – the plural is most noteworthy because it is exceptional - are mighty indeed, omnipotent, and they are true. It is a terrible thing to fall into those hands (Heb 10:31) but ever the height of blessedness to commend oneself into those hands."

16. THREE PICTURES OF THE GOSPEL

Pastor Ian had a weekend off and I filled in the gap taking the next passage as we worked our way through the letter to the Colossians.

Reading: Colossians 2: 6-12

Text: Colossians 2:13-15

[13] When you were dead in your sins and in the uncircumcision of your flesh, God made you alive with Christ. He forgave us all our sins, [14] having cancelled the charge of our legal indebtedness, which stood against us and condemned us; he has taken it away, nailing it to the cross. [15] And having disarmed the powers and authorities, he made a public spectacle of them, triumphing over them by the cross.

We are working our way through Colossians, though I will touch on these words, the text I have read is actually for next week's sermon from Ian. I was quite envious as it is one of my favourite verses because it is where the gospel of Christ is very clearly put forward in very powerful imagery. Today I am hoping at least to give a good foundation for his message next week as we look at what prompted Paul to write these words.

When Salah Abdesalam the last of the suspected Paris bombers was arrested in April this year, his lawyer said of him that he had the IQ of an empty ash tray. Compared to the five who took a tinnie from Melbourne to north Queensland with the hope of going to Indonesia and then to Syria, surely he was a genius! Yet, stupid as they were, one of them, Musa Cerantonio who was an outspoken cheerleader for ISIS, was described as someone who has inspired numerous foreign fighters to join jihadist groups in Syria. Forget the fact that they are Muslim, you just want to shout, look at the calibre of these men. Just who they are disqualifies them from being listened to. Anyone with a sound mind would have to run from them.

> **In Ephesus Paul attacks the messengers**
>
> - The heretics taught for financial reward 1 Tim 6:5; Tit 1:11
> - They deceived 2 Tim 3:13
> - They were hypocrites 2 Tim 3:5; Tit 1:16, 3:8-9
> - They argued over words not substance 1 Tim 1:4, 6; 4:2; 2 Tim 2:14, 16, 23; Tit 1:10; 3:9
> - There is a list of vices 1 Tim 1:9-10; 2 Tim 3:2-4
> - They had success among women 2 Tim 3:6

Paul took the exact same approach when he wrote to Timothy about the troubles in the church in Ephesus. He doesn't even bother to refute what they were saying. In my book, Introduction to the Pastoral Epistles, I give 26 pages to trying to determine what the heresy was and anybody's guess is probably as good as another's. He attacked the messengers because they don't deserve to be listened to irrespective of what they are saying. Look at them, who are they targeting as disciples? Rich young uneducated widows. Expose them for what they are; don't waste time on what they say. Sadly such men exist today, men who can even stand in a pulpit and say all things that are orthodox but at the heart they are rotten to the core.

Nature of the Colossian Heresy

```
CHRISTIANITY
Salvation through ----------|
Christ alone                |
                            |
JUDAISM          The Colossian heresy was an
Salvation through ----- amalgam of doctrines that
keeping the OT Law   did not reject Christ openly ------------|
                     but displaced His                        |
MYSTERY CULTS        preeminence and distorted                |
Salvation through ----- salvation.              Second-Century
special knowledge                               Gnosticism
                                                              |
GREEK PHILOSOPHY -------|                                     |
Angel worship                                                 |
Asceticism           Libertinism was not ---------------------|
Libertinism          addressed in Colossians, but
                     was found in later
                     Gnosticism
```

But in this letter separated only by a short time span and short distance from Timothy's, Paul tackles the wrong belief head on. Paul does not give it a name for us to hang a hat on but there is common enough agreement amongst the scholars to say that we what we are looking at was an amalgam of paganism, Judaism and Christianity and especially included aspects of what was probably an early form of Gnosticism. The name of this belief comes from the Greek word for knowledge. This belief was not known before Christianity yet it would gain such popularity that it has been described as a world viewpoint that would become as widely held as evolution is now.

Polycarp, a disciple of the Apostle John recounted how seriously he viewed this heresy. The story goes that, in Ephesus, John "once entered a bath to bathe; but, learning that Cerinthus was within, he sprang from the place and rushed out of the door, for he could not bear to remain under the same roof with him. And he advised those that were with him to do the same, saying, "Let us flee, lest the bath fall; for Cerinthus, the enemy of the truth, is within."" Gnosticism, though it still exists in its full blown form, it is rare now but aspects of its beliefs have cast a long shadow which affects us to this day, even pursuing us here to Tent Hill.

This damned heresy, and damned is not too strong a word to describe Gnosticism when you consider that Simon Magus of Acts Chapter 8, a man full of bitterness and captive to sin was one of the leaders. He was a man who thought God's gifts could be purchased with money. Gnosticism would take so many different forms that it was impossible to define it but, in whatever form, it would ridicule the thought of a divine redeemer. God was too holy to ever have created a sinful world, or ever to have anything to do with it. Between god and man they confidently asserted were a series of less and less divine beings and angels. The words thrones and powers from verses 10 and 15 are words used to name some of these intermediaries. The elemental spirits of verse eight and twenty are also part of their terminology. This was the world our God called good and our heavenly father tended it with such loving care that he fed the birds and saw when the least of them fell. Despite this, they said man's access to god was through worship and homage of these lesser beings and this could only be done through the possession of secret knowledge and through, as the case seems to be in Colossae, extreme denial of the body.

> IQ's of an empty ashtray not a modern phenominan
>
> Jesus said to his disciples, "I am come forth out of that first mystery, which is the last mystery, that is the four-and-twentieth mystery." And his disciples ... thought of that mystery, that it is the head of the universe and head of all existence; and they thought it is the completion of all completions ... that it surroundeth the First Commandment and the five Impressions and the Great Light and the Five Helpers and the whole Treasury of the Light. Extract from Pistis Sophia, a leading Gnostic work

My Jesus said simple but profound things like, "I am the light of the world." The Gnostics had Jesus saying things they thought were more profound and I will quote one example "Jesus said to his disciples, "I am come forth out of that first mystery, which is the last mystery, that is the four-and-twentieth mystery." And his disciples ... thought of that mystery, that it is the head of the universe and head of all existence; and they thought it is the completion of all completions ... that it surroundeth the First Commandment and the five Impressions and the Great Light and the Five Helpers and the whole Treasury of the Light". Well this is all in the calibre of empty ash trays and you would think what anywhere near rational person is going to fall for it, so where is this shadow?

One shadow is in trusting your eternal destiny to a spiritual encounter. They can be fairly easy to come by, look in the right crystal, smoke the right cigarettes, pop the right pill, play the right music, and twirl like dervish and you can be almost guaranteed one. It was no different then, there are even accounts in Ephesus of "mysteries" the word given to these encounters during the worship of the living Caesar. But then you are forced to create your beliefs and practices around your experiences. It will be a religion with you at the core and Jesus at best to the outside and as best as your spirit guide. Christianity can have very profound encounters with Jesus and his Father but there is a framework by which to judge it,

A second shadow says that I am too sinful to ever be able to be redeemed by a holy God. Surely we have heard that before. Imagine saying to an all knowing God who is offering you forgiveness, "If you only knew what I have done."

A third shadow is that I can lift myself up by my own bootstraps so that God has to accept me. I am not a bad person after all, I live a good life. Put me on the scales of justice and the good I have done far outweighs the bad.

A fourth shadow is that all I have to do is keep the outward ritual of the faith and that is enough. "Get done" when you are a teenager and everything is fine.

A fifth shadow is that there is no need to repent, we just had to reignite the divine spark which we do through freedom from ignorance.

Much of what I listed above, you will see in the new age movement. And over the years you will have seen some or all of the others. In verse eight, Paul likens people who teach such things to slave traders and meaning those that follow them are not liberated, but their captives. God could not bridge the gap between the worlds of spirit and flesh, the false Gnostics said. Jesus at best was an apparition who left no footprints when he walked on the sand and only appeared to die, mocking, not forgiving his executors. Paul's message to the Colossians and to us in Tent Hill is that it is not OK for Jesus to be marginalised, and he will not have his role as Lord and Saviour diminished. There is only Christ! Yes our Father is holy, and yes, we are sinful and, yes, there was a dividing wall between us that we could never cross, but no new age spirit guide is ever going to help us cross it. No spiritual encounter without Jesus at its centre will ever open our eyes to our loving and forgiving father.

But the scandal to the heretics is that everything that God is, was found in Jesus, because he was God himself, and as a real man and the only God walked and ate with sinful men. He showed us how to live and love and to forgive, and finally, he died a real death and was buried in a real tomb and a real but transformed body came out of that grave on the third day. There is no place in this for intermediaries, be they angels or saints or his mother. How can there be a place for them when we have been given the right to enter boldly into his presence? How can we spend time searching elsewhere for enlightenment when the king of this universe has promised to bring us fullness? Granted, we have only the down payment in this world but the one who promised has all the fullness of God and he has proven himself faithful.

But Ted, what about this dividing wall? How can a holy God put his hands around the shoulders of me a sinner and walk with me? I point you to baptism. When I was a young student in my first year of theological college we had a brilliant lecturer but be he was adamant in his belief that you must be baptised to be saved. I would hope on one hand that we know that just as the blood of sheep and goats could not wash away sins, neither will the depth of our baptistery free us from sin. It does not work ex opera operato, to quote the little Latin I know, which can be understood by some to mean get the ritual right, say the right words, and grace is imparted, you are set for life.

Yet equally we would not be true to the scriptures we hold as a certain guide if we do not take seriously its strong words about baptism. When Peter was asked (Acts 2:38) "What must we do to be saved" he replied "Repent and be baptised for the remission of your sins". When Ananias came to Paul he said to him (Acts 22:16) "And now what are you waiting for? Get up, be baptised and wash your sins away, calling on his name."

Our passage also speaks of Baptism in very strong terms, of us rising with Christ but it is in the context of one of three pictures of our redemption. The first is of circumcision. Presumably those that were troubling the church put an emphasis on this, probably as an initiation into their secret knowledge. Paul takes this idea saying "in him you were also circumcised with a circumcision not performed by human hands. Your whole self ruled by the flesh was put off when you were circumcised by Christ." A priest or a cult leader could only take a little bit, but God himself made a bigger and inward cut putting off the flesh that ruled us. In the third image everything that stood between us and the father was taken by him and nailed to the cross, not after we sorted ourselves out and made ourselves worthy, but when we were his enemies.

The second image of our redemption is baptism "having been buried with him in baptism, in which you were also raised with him through your faith in the working of God, who raised him from the dead". It is God the father who raises you from the dead through baptism. I do not pretend to understand what happens in baptism but my understanding, and it may well be very different to yours, is that there is a line drawn under your life when you, in faith identify with the crucified and risen Jesus. That there is something left behind in the baptistery, or the creek or the pool when you come out. There is little reproach to anyone in our society being baptised but there was back then. I saw it in India where we support Pastor Richard. There baptism can cost you family, inheritance and even life itself. But you will say to me, if God put off the flesh, and the imagery is like discarding clothing, why do I still battle with my old sinful nature. Paul acknowledges this in the next chapter where he deals with putting on a new self and clothing ourselves with the fruit of God's Spirit, the only attributes worthy of God's chosen, holy and dearly loved children. Of becoming such people who have earned the right to be listened to, because we show in our lives and bearing the God who lives in us.

In contrast, the heretics were in effect saying, go back in, drag it up, dry it off, pretty it up with some nice clothes of your own making and present it back to our better god and come explore the mysteries of the cosmos with us. Liberation they called it, Paul called it slavery. Finish the way you started Paul said "So then, just as you received Christ Jesus as Lord, continue to live your lives in him, rooted and built up in him, strengthened in the faith as you were taught, and overflowing with thankfulness."

The Colossian believers are reminded that there is only Jesus and in him they live and move and have their being. Only "in Christ", as a baby, a child, a man and finally on a cross is the fullness of God found by men and "in Christ" he shares this fullness with us. And as he was buried we were buried "with him" and as he was raised we were raised "with him" and made alive 'with him". And now being accepted we live "in him" and are built up "in him".

It is a gospel for all

The Gnostics reduced faith to a correct belief system and we are in danger of doing the same through seeing intellectual assent to a creed the being the same as faith. Let me tell you about two men, Bobby and Nicholas, who were not wise and who were not initiated into deep secrets, indeed they never could be.

Bobby is shown here with Phil. Phil has had his eyes surgically removed and both these old men had a dreadful medical condition before they were 10. Bobby had a stroke. Here the two are working together making products for me. Bobby with his withered arm and damaged brain is lining the timber up for Phil to drill. They made a good team. Bobby would always say to me on the Monday how sorry he was that he had not been at work but he had been sick. You see Bobby didn't understand what a weekend was and if you were not at work then you had to have been sick. One day at work he told me that pastor told him he had a home in heaven and you could just see that he believed it. I have promised him an arm wrestle on the other side.

Nicholas had a profound intellectual disability. When he died in his early thirties his believing mother had never even heard him say, "Mum". In his teens he was at a Bible study and his mother happened to be out of the room. The minister asked, "How can we be saved?" Nicholas said clearly, "By the Holy Spirit".

No, their IQ was not high and they would never gather disciples to themselves, neither could they ever give intellectual assent to a creed. But they possessed what is needed and with such our Lord is pleased to dwell with and in and call his own. Such men can know the treasures of the mystery of God. How could we not but love him too?

17. I WANT A V12 E TYPE JAGUAR

Reading: Psalm 37

*¹ **Do not fret** because of those who are evil or be envious of those who do wrong; ² for like the grass they will soon wither, like green plants they will soon die away.*

³ Trust in the LORD and do good; dwell in the land and enjoy safe pasture. ⁴ Take delight in the LORD, and he will give you the desires of your heart.

⁵ Commit your way to the LORD; trust in him and he will do this: ⁶ He will make your righteous reward shine like the dawn, your vindication like the noonday sun.

⁷ Be still before the LORD and wait patiently for him; ***do not fret*** *when people succeed in their ways, when they carry out their wicked schemes.*

⁸ Refrain from anger and turn from wrath; ***do not fret*** *- it leads only to evil. ⁹ For those who are evil will be destroyed, but those who hope in the LORD will inherit the land.*

¹⁰ A little while, and the wicked will be no more; though you look for them, they will not be found. ¹¹ But the meek will inherit the land and enjoy peace and prosperity.

> **Text:** Psalm 37:37
>
> Consider the blameless, observe the upright; a future awaits those who seek peace.

Text: Psalm 37:37

Consider the blameless, observe the upright; a future awaits those who seek peace.

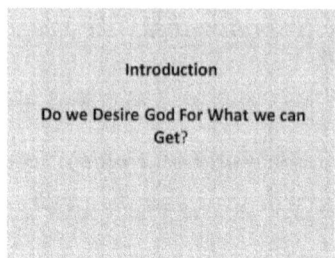

Introduction: Do We Desire God For What we can Get

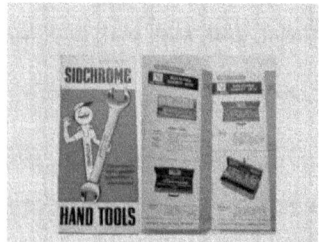

When I was an apprentice motor mechanic I had, as you would expect, a set of tradesman's tools, all Sidchrome and as the older ones here may recall, their advertisement of the time said, "You canna hand a man a grander spanner, than a Sidchrome, that's the brand the experts use". As we owned British vehicles, naturally, I had a full set of Whitworth spanners to fit the odd size nuts and bolts they used. Of course they are useless now unless you are working on old British equipment. Somewhat reluctantly, I gave them to David Pederson at our church, because that is exactly what he does. But it was given with one condition.

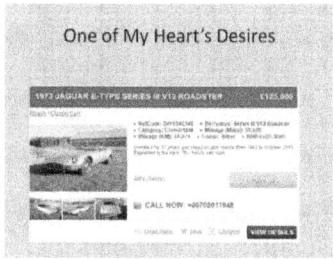

But before I tell you that condition, let me ask you, what is the desire of your heart? Our reading said in verse 4, "Take delight in the LORD, and he **will** give you the desires of your heart." So, what are the desires of your heart, we all have them. I don't think I have that many now in my older age but let me tell you of one I still have. Sadly it is a sign of my lack of sanctification. I would like to own V12 E Type Jaguar!! For the younger ones among you, it is a sports car built in England in the 1960's and 70's. It is probably the most beautiful car ever built and, unfortunately, they are very expensive. But you need Whitworth spanners to work on one and that condition that accompanied the gift of spanners was that, when there is an E Type parked in my garage the spanners come back! Now, I have to tell you also, despite what that verse says about God giving me the desires of my heart I know I will never own one and that David's possession of those spanners is very safe. And that is despite delighting myself in the Lord for over 40 years.

Now I expect that the delights of your heart are far more practical than mine but will they all be granted for all of that? There are some who will tell you that it is only your lack of faith that keeps you from them! Let me tell you about the mother in law of my good friend Noe Galzote, a remarkable pastor in the Philippines. She is a woman who is blameless and upright. Corrupt city officials grabbed the land she and the other slum dwellers were living on for over 50 years and tried to sell it to a developer. Her heart's desire is not for an expensive and totally impractical classic car in the garage but for a home and to live in peace. Tragically her reality is that she has been advised that she shouldn't go out alone as opposing such people can be fatal! She has come face to face with the people envisaged in verse one, "**Do not fret** because of those who are evil or be envious of those who do wrong". At 75 and a strong believer, she knows that the second part of that verse "for like the grass they will soon wither, like green plants they will soon die away" is not a threat to the ungodly but a promise to us all, righteous or evil.

> Point 1.
> What Path Have you Been Called to Walk?

Point 1. What Path have you been called to Walk

Our own nation is blessed with not having the open corruption and unrestrained evil of many countries that can even see you turned out of your home. But there is another evil, in that the heart's desire of many for home ownership is now out of the reach through a market being distorted by the prosperous. For some, at least, the question of where that wealth came from is questionable. How many books are there in the Bible, 66? Perhaps it is 67, the last is the unwritten Book of Providence and our Psalm is an exposition of some of its hardest chapters "the advancement of the wicked and the disgrace of the righteous" as one commentator said. "Life is what happens when you are making other plans," so John Lennon said, and in the face of life we could easily murmur and lose our trust in the Lord. David, with the hindsight of old age, three times in our reading, gives the same advice, "Do not fret."

But the Psalmist David also knew that alongside the life of disappointment and sorrow can be a life of peace and prosperity, where things just fall into place without striving, like an inheritance coming in due time. Yes, even as a vindication of the faith and trust placed in the Lord, the meek will inherit the land and enjoy peace and prosperity. This Psalm is not a magical formula on how to get what you want from life, if you do "such and such" a thing then God will do what you want him to do. The message is very simple, "faithfulness will yield the reward of a life well lived." I don't know which of the two paths you have been called to walk, a path if not of tears at least of frustration or a path of joy, most likely it is a mixture of both and some here would have unresolved questions over the way people have dealt with you.

The sin, not the prosperity of evil men should grieve the righteous.

The Old Testament is full of examples of people taking issue with God and questioning him but it is always something that is worked through. If you don't, it eventually leads to the questioning of God's power and denying his rule over this world. As Spurgeon said when he preached on this psalm "Grieving at their success leads to other evil feelings and makes us like them". No, the sin, not the prosperity of evil men should grieve the righteous. Why should we be filled with anger and resentment at them and begrudge them their short lived gain. They have chosen something as short lived, and ultimately with as much value as the grass of the field. We, instead, have been given the promise of friendship with our maker and an eternal inheritance beyond cost? No, we shouldn't fret but rather we should pity their blindness.

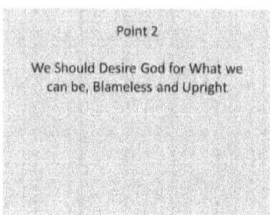

Point 2
We Should Desire God for What we can be, Blameless and Upright

Point 2. We Should Desire God for What we can be, Blameless and Upright

My friends, you and I are not called to bring God's vengeance on the ungodly nor on the other hand are we called, as testament to our great faith, to have E Types parked in our garage. Neither are we called to live a life directed entirely by our own choosing and ability and strength. Instead, we are simply called to live a life that is blameless and upright, and to do it before God in the face of a world that ignores or opposes him. We are called to have a life that sets us apart, consider the blameless, observe the upright.

Where our life should be focused

Trust in the LORD v 3&5
Take delight in the LORD v4
Commit your way to the LORD v5
Be still before the LORD v7
Hope in the LORD v8

In our reading the Psalmist tells us where our life should be focused:

Trust in the LORD v 3&5
Take delight in the LORD v4
Commit your way to the LORD v5
Be still before the LORD v7
Hope in the LORD v8

In none of these commands does it say "God", like "hope in God". That can mean different things to different people. It can be almost meaningless and even blasphemous in its irreverence, "May the force be with you", or "the big guy upstairs". This is not same vague nameless thing like having your stars aligned in the right way. Nor is a matter of your home having good feng shui or being born on auspicious days. Your God is not an anonymous force; your God has a name and he made it known to the Jews by four letters YHWH, a word that our translations render as the LORD. When you give your name to someone you are not standing aloof, you make yourself known to them; in a way it is to hand oneself over by becoming accessible, capable of being known more intimately and addressed personally. How that word is pronounced has been lost and theologians argue about its origins but "we are left with the echoes of a revelation that was as sincere and confidential as the word abba: daddy."

Do you know this God who has a name? He knows your name, he knew you when you were formed in your mother's womb. His grace and love has preserved you to this day. He wants you to know him as a friend. He wants you to delight in him just as he wants to delight in you and make you blameless and upright. Delight in him so we can have and E Type in the garage or a roof over your head? No, simply because he should be the object of our delight because he is worthy of that delight. The same God who appeared to Moses in the burning bush and revealed his name to him is the same one who lived among men with a name Jesus, but its significance is not obscured in the mist of time. Its meaning was very clear, "He will save his people from their sins".

"Jesus is Lord" was probably the earliest creed of the Christian church. The commitment involved in believing that "Jesus is Lord" was not just confined to outward religious actions like an hour a week in church; it also meant a different life style. The theologian and church historian, FF Bruce, said of the first believers, that the ethical requirements of the Christian faith "were most earnestly inculcated (drummed in) in new converts" and for the most part they were accepted and put into practice". Some Gentile converts "may have lived very reprehensible lives", but on embracing the Christian message they did so "with the assurance that God in Christ had wiped out their past misdeeds"(Bruce: Spreading Flame 199). It should be no different today as we strive to live blameless and upright lives.

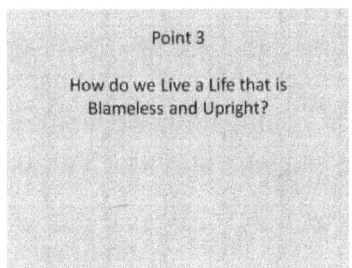

Point 3, How do we Live a Life that is Blameless and Upright?

My friends, if you ask "What do we do so we can live a life that is blameless and upright", my answer is, "It is much the same as for the Old Testament saints but with one very big difference." Time and time again a priest had to go before God with the blood of sheep and goats to wipe away the past. Of course it could never could it wipe away sin except that it looked forward to the cross of Jesus where once and for all our sin and the sin of the Old Testament saints who lived by faith, just as we do, was dealt with. Look at those five commands again:

There all require knowing your God

Trust in the LORD v 3&5
Take delight in the LORD v4
Commit your way to the LORD v5
Be still before the LORD v7
Hope in the LORD v8

Trust in the LORD v 3&5
Take delight in the LORD v4
Commit your way to the LORD v5
Be still before the LORD v7
Hope in the LORD v8

There is really not much "doing" in any of this, but there is a lot of "knowing" and it can involve a lot of living in a degree of uncertainty. What is there to do? The thing which you could never do has been done for you. When you confessed Jesus is

Lord your sins were forgiven. You never were worthy, you never will be worthy but that God who has a name and knows your name says "learn of me". He says throw your lot in with mine, commit your way to me and let's go on a journey together. In the first trial of adversity he will prove himself trustworthy and next time around it is so much easier to say, "We can do this." Each time, as you contemplate the many ways that he shows his love to you, it becomes natural to delight in him and be still before him. As for hope, Jesus wants to teach you to pass your days on earth but to live as citizens of heaven. This world is not our home, but it will be our inheritance.

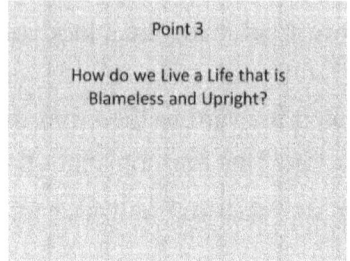

Point 4: What future awaits the blameless and upright who seek peace?

What future awaits the blameless and upright who seek peace? I was visiting my 98 year old mother a few weeks back at Tabeel in Laidley. My mother's mind has been elsewhere for a few years now. I asked her how she was, not expecting a coherent answer, but in a moment of lucidity said, "How do you think I feel sitting here without a future!" "Mum, you do have a future, Jesus will come and take you to himself and you will be with him forever", "Yes I do have that." And with that she went back to that place in her mind she has been these last years. For the blameless and the upright, just like the wicked, their lives are like grass and green plants but a future remains for them when all has passed away.

Is "pie in the sky" all you can give me? No, but it is all I can guarantee you as none of us are promised tomorrow. But God's word assures us that if you confess that Jesus is LORD your sins are forgiven and Jesus has prepared a place in heaven for you. Fortunately, the odds are pretty good that we will live long enough for us to know our LORD well and to learn to delight in him. Time will give us the opportunity to strive to be blameless and upright. Are there blessings in this world too? Sure, too many to count. For starters, a life walked hand in hand with this world's creator, someone to talk to in all of life's situations, someone who will order the circumstances of your life and someone who will help in your time of need. Considering this, who would not want to be blameless and upright.

Conclusion

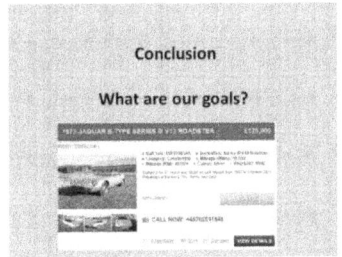

On Friday, our loan broker sent me a circular email saying "Whatever's on your wish list, ask us about financing it." I replied, "V12 E Type Jag? Even you are not that good Tim!" "Good to have goals", he replied. Well I am not really working on that one. We are challenged to have a goal of something of far more value, something that is beyond cost, to be blameless and upright. That is something that everyone here should have as a goal and should all be working on. Working? Not the right word I know, rather knowing the one who should be the delight of our heart.

18. JOB'S MISERABLE COMFORTERS

This sermon started life in Tent Hill and came out of my studies for my Master of Theology. In 2016 I visited friends in the Philippines and was asked to preach in a village church near Clarke Air Base. It was substantially reworked. A group walked 14 km just to get to hear me and had to walk 14 back uphill. I could feel the words of this sermon dropping between the pulpit and the first row but my Friend. Noe Galzote's translation gave some life.

Afterwards the Pastor of the group that walked the 14 km thanked me for the sermon. I said that I felt that I had missed things entirely. He said "No, you were just telling us things we had never heard before. We had always been taught that if you were suffering you must have sinned. Now we must go and consider these things."

Reading: Job Chapter 4

Ville du Havre – in Nov 1873 she sunk in two minutes after colliding with clipper Lock Earn with loss of 226 lives

The hymn "It is well with my soul" that was sung may not be familiar to you but it is a much loved hymn in Australia. It was written a long time ago by Horatio Spafford a Chicago businessman. All of the older hymn tunes have names and the tune we sing this hymn to is called *Ville du Havre*, after one of the largest ships crossing the Atlantic at the time. On a bright starry night on the 22nd November 1873 she was struck amidships by the iron sailing ship Loch Earn and in 12 minutes she went under taking 226 of the 313 people on board to their death. Among the dead were the four daughters of Horatio Spafford and a group of his friends.

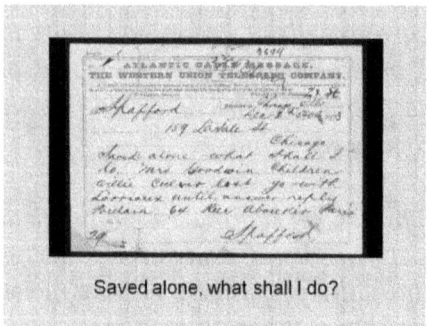

Saved alone, what shall I do?

Horatio had been detained on business in Chicago and couldn't travel with the family. On December 1st he received a telegram from his wife, "Saved alone. What shall I do"? What Horatio did was to write this hymn. Horatio had been a very wealthy man but it did not insulate him from tragedy. His 2 year old son had died two years previously and, in the same year, many of the properties he owned in Chicago burnt in a great fire. His remaining business interests were severely hit by an economic downturn in 1873. He went on to have three more children, two daughters and a son. The son died at the age of four of scarlet fever. In the midst of so much suffering, what did his church do? Draw close to him and support and comfort him? No! While we in 2016 sing this hymn and take great comfort from his response to suffering, his church family looked at his misfortune as divine punishment, justly dealt out upon a sinner. Their theology taught them that if God's favour rested upon a person they would prosper. Heaven knows there are many now who think similarly. How do you look upon the suffering of people who name Christ as their own?

A couple of years ago when I was doing some study for a university course I spent a lot time in the book of Job. As I contemplated Job I came to the conclusion that, despite the 3000+ years that have passed the more things change, the more they stay the same.

"My wife doesn't understand me any longer," so a certain man complained. "She is not as pretty as when we first got married, but my neighbour's wife, well she understands me and she is a lot prettier, and she thinks the same way about me. But I think I might talk to my three friends before I – well you know."

What does the priest say?

He went to his friend the priest and told him what he was considering and the answer was, "The Law of Moses says, "Thou shall not commit adultery" and it is your duty to obey". But this man said "I am not certain there is a God so why should I put my happiness ahead of what might just be a myth" so he ignored the priest's advice.

What does the prophet say?

He then went to see his friend the prophet and told him what his intensions were. The prophet was shocked and replied, "God says not to commit adultery and if you break his law it will stop raining, the creek will stop running, your wells will dry up, you will have pests and weeds in your crops and you will sell them for a bad price. The man thought for a while and said "That exactly what has been happening to the God fearing farmers in our valley for the last 100 years, nothing changes". So he says, "I am not convinced".

What does the wise man say?

He then went to see his friend the wise man and he told him, "Have you taken complete leave of your senses. You would not listen to God's Law, you would not listen to God's prophet well listen to some reason. Don't you know in the divorce settlement your wife will take 70% of everything you own, she will take half your superannuation, she will move away and marry again, you will see the children you love one week a year. They will call someone else "dad" but you will still pay all their expenses till they are 25. Are you a complete fool." I expect divorce law is very different in the Philippines

I don't know what I saw in her

Suddenly the strength of the three arguments brings him to his senses and says to himself, "Whatever did I see in my neighbour's wife?"

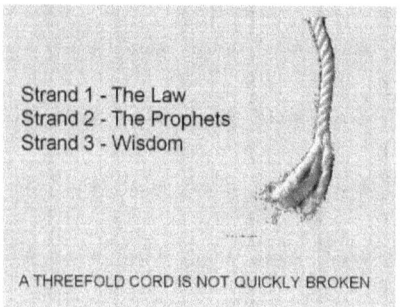

A THREEFOLD CORD IS NOT QUICKLY BROKEN

Ecclesiastes 4:12 says "and though one might prevail against another, two will withstand one. A threefold cord is not quickly broken". And here we have the threefold cord that God gave his people Israel, the cords of the Law, the prophets and of wisdom, and we see wisdom in Proverbs and Ecclesiastes and Job and that is where we are headed. The divorce advice was what our family solicitor would tell the men who would come to him, and not too many men initiated a divorce. Sadly, the women would start right away. Wisdom is universal and in the Old Testament times there was a whole body of literature in surrounding nations that had similarities with Israel's wisdom, but Israel's wisdom was different, they combined wisdom with the fear of the Lord and that is very, very powerful. But false wisdom without correctly discerning the ways of God is a dangerous thing and will take us places we were never meant to go.

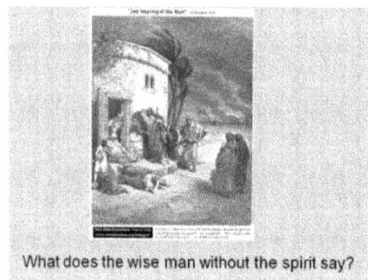

What does the wise man without the spirit say?

Job's setting, if not its date of writing, is the "patriarchal, or better, pre-patriarchal world". Job presents a world before God's self revelation in the exodus and the covenant, and any advanced idea of the Spirit. It is set in a time when people are "attempting to discover the purpose of life and the nature of God." All Abraham had was a simple command, "walk before me and be holy" but God gave him no text book on how to do it. That was in a time before the Law and now we live in a time when the Law is passed. We are given one Law, the Law of Christ, to love God with all our hearts and our neighbour as ourselves. It is scaringly like the command to walk before God and be holy.

We spend our lifetime attempting to discover the purpose of life and the nature of God. We live a life of discovery. Ask any of the old members here how much their theology has changed since their youth. Probably not much, in my church they would be Baptist through and through, and there is nothing wrong with that. But ask these same people how much they have discovered about God, and his ways, and his purposes since they were young, I think they will say that they are not the people they were when they were young. Young people, you are on the beginning of a road of discovery. It can be a rough road at times, but hang in for the ride, it can be exciting and the rewards along the way are great.

Let's return to Job, who like Horatio Spafford, lost everything and everybody, except his wife and that is another matter. While she is saying, "Curse God and die," I think I can hear him say "only lose only 70% in a divorce that might be a good deal". There he is sitting in the dust, his wife berating him and his three friends, Eliphaz, Bildad and Zophar and a young man he doesn't know Elihu come to visit him. What words of comfort do they have? "Job you are a sinner, in fact, not only are you a sinner but you're are a dreadful sinner and we know this without any doubt". Eliphaz the leader of the three friends tells Job, "We know that life is simply "cash register justice"". The friends had their own three strand cord by which to judge Job.

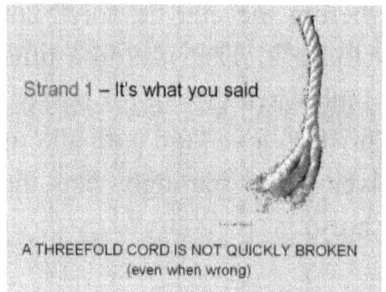

The first strand 4:3-5 - Job, this is exactly what you were telling everyone who would find themselves in trouble. No doubt Job was thinking, "Thank God for the journey of discovery, I would never say that again without good cause," and I say thank God for the journey of discovery.

The second strand 4:6-8 – Job you know it has never been otherwise – only sinners suffer. It is a circular argument that refuses to look at the facts. It didn't square with the history of Israel. You know it doesn't square with life 5

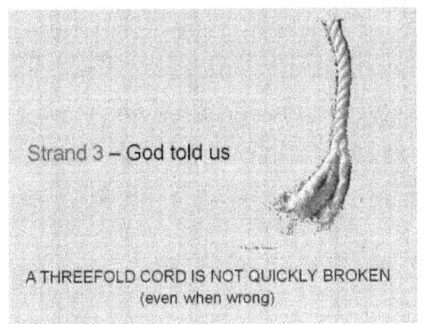

The third strand 4:12-21 – "God told me". How many times have you heard people say "God has told me". How do you argue against that, imagine my pastor or your pastor coming to the deacons and elders meeting and saying, "God has told me we have to do such and such, let's take a vote". You are seen as arguing against God if you say "No" and questioned whether God had truly spoken. The Old Testament prophets spoke as though they stood in God's presence and could say, "Thus says the Lord" but Eliphaz only glimpsed something spirit-like and he only heard it indistinctly. He heightens the mystical quality of his encounter with God by heaping together rare technical and indeterminate words, 15 A spirit glided past my face; the hair of my flesh bristled. 16 it stood still, but I could not discern its appearance. A form was before my eyes; there was silence, then I heard a voice It is in the realms of the spooky yet despite its ethereal nature Eliphaz considers his encounter as authoritative but it was very wrong.

Despite the privileged position he claimed as a recipient of divine secrets, Eliphaz has no idea of the divine wager of Chapters 1 and 2. One commentator described Eliphaz as "a dangerous man" because he speaks the truth at the wrong time and in the wrong spirit. He is far more dangerous because he does speak the truth about the holiness of God (4:17-21) without speaking the truth about Job. Eliphaz's perceived superior knowledge and irrefutable theology "had dried up the springs of true sympathy". He claims God's authority and a Spirit encounter for his failure to show that deep love to Job characterised in the Hebrew word . That word is virtually untranslatable but loving kindness is probably the closest in English

The prophetic along with prophetic abuses was a major factor for good and ill in Israel's history and its abuse is still a problem today. Don't misunderstand me, I am not one to denounce a deep and profound encounter with the father through his Spirit, don't think that for a moment, but we can give these encounters far too much importance. Let me give you an example:

Pastor John Kilpatrick

In about 1998 I went to Pensacola in Florida USA to witness a revival that was occurring there. To see people queuing for hours to get a seat in the church and to witness men and women running to the front of the church to give their lives to Jesus is a deeply moving thing experience. The meetings were held in incredible order but at the altar call there was pandemonium. The assistant pastor told us that many of them were coming from the vilest sin and that the Devil did not give them up easily. After one of the services I was standing at the back of the church talking with friends, and up the aisle staggered the head pastor like a drunken man. He had been the model of decorum during the service but now anything but, and he was laying hands on people and praying for them. I said a silent prayer of my own "Lord, don't let him anywhere near me". With that he made a line straight for me and prayed a prayer that asked for deliverance from matters known in that room only to God and me. It was a matter I was powerless to do anything about. Within two months it was resolved favourably for me.

What are we to conclude then, that out pastor in our little country church has not earned his wages unless he staggers down the aisle every Sunday laying hands on people and makes powerful prayers that come from the father's heart and changes lives? Rather think of Luke 2:19 but Mary treasured all these words and pondered them in her heart. Some of the things that have happened to us, and young people, the things that will happen to you are just like that. Don't try to understand them, don't make them a pattern for your life, just ponder and treasure them.

No, this three strand rope was just an illusion of Eliphaz's own imagination, a construct to make sense of his universe so he did not have to face difficult questions for which there will be no answers in this world.

ELIHU THE SAGE

In Chapter 32 we are introduced to Elihu. This young upstart listened to the three friends with disgust. These old men thought they were wise but Elihu claimed that the insight given by the Spirit in a person is of more value than that handed down from an elder. And he had the Spirit in such force in him that, like a wine skin, if he could not release the pressure by speaking God's words, he would simply explode. God has told me "Job you are a sinner".

Elihu considered himself as rational and patient, (32:6-22). He thought that his wisdom was so great it enables him to be considered a sage, wise enough to teach even Job (32-6-9). But that is not what the author of the book wants us to see. Despite Elihu's own opinion that he is moved by the Spirit, the writer shows him moved by anger. Four times in 32:1-5 the story teller stresses Elihu's anger so we can see the true nature of his words. This wouldn't have been seen by the three friends and Job and he would have looked so spiritual. God has told me, God has told me, but by showing us his motives, the storyteller allows us to question if Elihu was indeed speaking by the Spirit for God at all. Elihu judgement of Job as wicked (34:36) is completely the opposite of God's (1:8, 2:3). Elihu had claimed to have perfect knowledge (36:4), just like God but his knowledge was incomplete and it is Job who is pronounced as having spoken what was right about God (42:7, 8). Elihu's spirit-empowered judgement about Job, coming from "complete knowledge", was just nonsense.

Let's try and pull this together. It is well over three thousand years since Job sat in the dust looking for friends but finding theologians. Despite that we still have people saying, "God has told me," when God has been silent. To say God has told me is very different to saying, I have a strong impression. It is only wisdom rooted in the fear of God that can help us sort which impression is from him and which has come from us and which was lunch disagreeing with us.

The safest way forward is the long journey of discovery of our God and not trying to take shortcuts through undue trust and reliance on personal revelations. Our experiences have been a blessing but much should remain hidden in our heart rather than being a template for nor normal life.

Let me return to Horatio Spafford. Job was honest with God and told him exactly what he thought. "In a court of law you would be found unjust," he hurled back at his maker. But Horatio's so called friends were no better than Job's friends and would not let him keep his integrity and grieve and perhaps Horatio himself did not let that bucket load of grief empty itself. I expect that this is a large part of the reason he later adopted some very strange beliefs and practices. For all of that he developed a powerful and much needed ministry of compassion in Jerusalem feeding the needy Jew, Christian and Muslim freely. Just as God was pleased with the heretic Job as against the theologians, in the end God may well have been better pleased with Horatio than those whose doctrine was pure but whose lives caused no one to bless God.

So let's go from here with a sense of expectancy of where our journey of discovery will take us. May we be full of compassion and mercy and judge no one, for Lord, if you judged us, who would stand?

19. BEWARE THE IDES OF MARCH

In the interim period between appointing a new senior pastor, our youth pastor, Tim, had taken on more of the preaching. And started a series on Philippians. He had to attend a training course on how to be a marriage celebrant so had no time to prepare the sermon. It fell to me to take the next passage

Reading: Phil. 3:12-21 *[12]Not that I have already obtained all this, or have already arrived at my goal, but I press on to take hold of that for which Christ Jesus took hold of me. [13]Brothers and sisters, I do not consider myself yet to have taken hold of it. But one thing I do: Forgetting what is behind and straining toward what is ahead, [14]I press on toward the goal to win the prize for which God has called me heavenward in Christ Jesus. [15]All of us, then, who are mature should take such a view of things. And if on some point you think differently, that too God will make clear to you. [16]Only let us live up to what we have already attained. [17]Join together in following my example, brothers and sisters, and just as you have us as a model, keep your eyes on those who live as we do. [18]For, as I have often told you before and now tell you again even with tears, many live as enemies of the cross of Christ. [19]Their destiny is destruction, their god is their stomach, and their glory is in their shame. Their mind is set on earthly things. [20]But our citizenship is in heaven. And we eagerly await a Savior from there, the LORD Jesus Christ, [21]who, by the power that enables him to bring everything under his control, will transform our lowly bodies so that they will be like his glorious body.*

Text: Phil. 3: [18]For, as I have often told you before and now tell you again even with tears, many live as enemies of the cross of Christ. [19]Their destiny is destruction, their god is their stomach, and their glory is in their shame. Their mind is set on earthly things. [20]But our citizenship is in heaven. And we eagerly await a Savior from there, the LORD Jesus Christ, [21]who, by the power that enables him to bring everything under his control, will transform our lowly bodies so that they will be like his glorious body.

Did you know that last Wednesday was the Ides of March? Now, if you are looking at me a bit strange and wondering what he is going on about, you obviously didn't study William Shakespeare's play, *Julius Caesar* at high school – "Beware the Ides of March", "Et tu, Brute", "Friends Romans Countrymen, lend me your ears" "Yon Cassius has a lean and hungry look" – he obviously didn't marry a Tenthill girl. I even remember one portion from Act 4 scene 3 when the ghost of Caesar appears to Brutus at night

Enter the Ghost of CAESAR

How ill this taper burns! Ha! who comes here?
I think it is the weakness of mine eyes
That shapes this monstrous apparition.
It comes upon me. Art thou any thing?
Art thou some god, some angel, or some devil,
That makest my blood cold and my hair to stare?
Speak to me what thou art.
GHOST
Thy evil spirit, Brutus.
BRUTUS

Why comest thou?

GHOST
To tell thee thou shalt see me at Philippi.

BRUTUS
Well; then I shall see thee again?

GHOST
Ay, at Philippi.

Battle of Philippi, October 42 BC

The death of Julius Caesar on the Ides of March, 44 BC set in place a civil war with Octavian and Mark Anthony on one side and the conspirators led by Brutus and Cassius. The showdown was at Phillipi. Octavian and Mark Anthony had 19 legions and 33,000 cavalry and Brutus and the rest had 17 legions and 17,000 cavalry and mounted bowmen. Now a legion at that time was about 3000 men. If at full strength, (and the assassins side was depleted) that would have given something like 90,000 facing off against 68,000. Tactics, not numbers won the battles in ancient times. The battle at Philippi, which was one of the greatest in antiquity, resulted in close combat between two armies of well-trained veterans. The historians said that arrows or javelins were largely ignored, and the soldiers, packed into solid ranks, fought face-to-face with their swords, and the slaughter was terrible. Brutal as that was, in ancient time the butchers bill really started to tally up when one side broke ranks and fled the field. You will remember the armour of God from Ephesians, it only protects when you are squaring off against the enemy.

Memorial Arch in Philippi to commemorate the battle

Mark Anthony and Octavian won and Octavian, the legal heir of Julius Caesar went on to became Augustus and would, unknowingly, set in place "the fullness of time" which enabled the gospel to grow and advance so quickly. When the dust settles, what do you do with an army that big and wants to be paid? Simple, kick any local Macedonians off their land and settle those and later veterans there in a Roman colony. Their military history was just outside of living memory but they all knew about it and were proud of it and there were reminders of it all over the city. The biggest reminder that no one could escape was their status, their city was considered an extension of Rome, not of the empire but of the capital with all the benefits that went with Roman citizenship that were denied to almost all. Even Paul would boast of citizenship by birth.

Imagine you were there standing in the ranks on morning of the battle at Philippi, can you imagine the stirring speeches that would have been delivered? We know from the last World War with the speeches of King George 6th and Winston Churchill how important the right message delivered in the right way can be to carry a people and an army facing overwhelming odds. The ancients understood this too. Julius Caesar took two years off conquering the world to study rhetoric, so he could inspire his army and the populous. In ancient Greek, let alone Latin, there are over 50 recorded speeches of generals to their troops and, invariably, it included

Contents of General's Addresses to troops
- The ancestry of the soldiers or general
- The command not to disgrace their heritage
- A comparison of the forces
- A statement that in war, valour not numbers prevail
- The promise that the most magnificent prizes await the victor
- The claim that the auspices are favorable, the gods are our allies

The ancestry of the soldiers or general
The command not to disgrace their heritage
A comparison of the forces
A statement that in war, valour not numbers prevail

The promise that the most magnificent prizes await the victor
The claim that the auspices are favorable, the gods are our allies

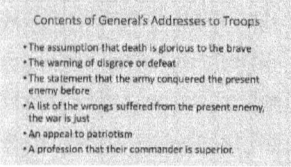

The assumption that death is glorious to the brave
The warning of disgrace or defeat
The statement that the army conquered the present enemy before
A list of the wrongs suffered from the present enemy, the war is just
An appeal to patriotism
A profession that their commander is superior.

For over 130 years most of these very same things have been spoken from this church's pulpit and will continue to be spoken to the soldiers of the cross who are involved in a civil war. And it is no coincidence that pastors, past, present and future would have often turned to the book of Philippians for these themes. If I may quote a scholar "Paul draft[ed] his letter in a rhetorical arrangement similar to the historical reports of commander's speeches to his assembled troops before battle. Not only does the vocabulary of Paul's ethical commands parallel the general's harangues, as has been previously pointed out by Biblical scholarship, but in Paul's letter one also finds correspondences to the three largest motifs of the general's speeches: the objective of the war, the confidence for victory and the rewards for courage and obedience. The major unified theme of Philippians is the mutual military-partnership for the advance of the gospel in a hostile context (Phil. 1:7-12; 1:20; 2:19-24; 2:25-30; 3:12-15; 4:3; 4:10-19)."

If Paul knew this church intimately and was writing to Tenthill he would write in terms that are familiar to us. He might talk about the GPS system in Barry's tractor that receives guidance from the heavens that allows him to plough a straight furrow. He could then liken that to the guidance we can receive from the heavenly GPS, God's Positioning System which enable us to live a straight life. Likewise, when Paul wrote to Philippi he used terminology and concepts that tapped into the deepest part of their consciousness of who they were as a people and what made them different to others.

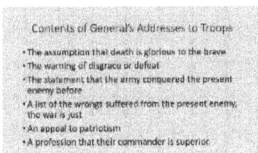

An army without its officers can quickly descend into a rabble. But an army with the right commander is formidable. Wellington said of Napoleon that when he was on the field of battle it was equal to another 40,000 men. When you read commentaries on 1 Timothy and it comes to the discussion of the qualifications of elders, the officers of the church (if you wish to call it that) it invariably comes around to discussing Onasander's book, *The General*. It is one of the most important treatises on ancient military matters and provides information not commonly available in other ancient works on Greek military tactics. There are very close parallels between his description of the ideal general who is to be a model for his troops and of an elder. By contrast, if you read any Australian World War Two history, you will soon learn how the troops despised General Blamey. Kenneth Slessor (I had to learn his Two Chronometers poem at school) wrote a poem about him. He starts by saying:

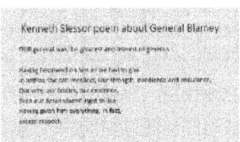

OUR general was the greatest and bravest of generals.
He goes on to say

Having bestowed on him all we had to give
In battles few can recollect, Our strength, obedience and endurance,
Our wits, our bodies, our existence,
Even our descendants' right to live—
Having given him everything, in fact,
Except respect.

Here we take up our text where Paul, like a general, is encouraging the citizen soldiers by reminding them of the rewards for courage and obedience. For 2000 years the church has existed with one eye on Jesus and one eye on those who strove to live by the example that had been set for them by the leaders of the previous generation. The qualities that make a good leader in the army and the church are not "secret men's business" and, dare I say, "secret women's business." Paul addresses brothers and sisters on equal footing here. Onasanders and Paul's requirements looked at the character of leaders but in our passage, the apostle points to the actions and the focus of leaders, but not just leaders but anyone who would call themselves mature in the faith.

In a general way Paul wanted the Philippian church to imitate him and not just the church in Philippi but all the churches he founded – we see the same command to the Corinthians (11;1). Well if you were very spiritual you might say, I want to imitate Christ, not man and that is good, but it is easier said than done. We have the four gospels now with all that the Good Lord has decided we need to know about Jesus, but those Philippians didn't have that though they probably had stories we don't have. But even then, with our fuller knowledge of Jesus, how much of his life can I imitate? I can't raise the dead or give sight to the blind or heal the sick. I definitely can't sway a crowd with powerful and profound preaching or come up with a quick profound answer to critics of the faith. I can attempt to live out the ethical commands of loving mercy and being forgiving but what we all need is to see this lived out in front of us. We need to be able to say, "The life that Jesus wants me to live can be done because I have seen it with my own eyes." We need people who will inspire us to feats and actions we never could have reached by ourselves. The Philippians had this in Paul and they took note and they gave him everything including respect. Paul has long since gone but he had the wisdom to say, "and just as you have us as a model, keep your eyes on those who live as we do."

But in verses 15-17 Paul wants us to follow his example in a very specific way because in the preceding three verses he is talking about his bold proclamation of the gospel. Paul presented himself in these verses as a soldier who is pursuing his enemies with the gospel. He is pressing on and straining. He is not resting in past victories or turning his back to the present challenge. He is doing this in the hope of capturing some for the good news in just the same way he was pursued and captured by Christ. In his fight Paul has an eye on the reward the commanding general gives at the end of the war, and, for this old seasoned campaigner, it is the resurrection and face to face knowledge of his Lord. His prize is not in his hands yet, but he can see it and he knows what is needed to grasp it. "I press on to take hold of that for which Christ Jesus took hold of me."

Paul told the Philippians that the way he sees things isn't something unique and just available for apostles. To quote again, "The book of Philippians challenges the contemporary self-centred prosperity culture of the church to take risks and make sacrifices for the proclamation of Christ to unbelievers, sacrifices, which are supremely compensated by a life for the glory of Christ and the surpassing promise of the enjoyment of the glory of God in His Son Christ Jesus." He tells them, "You think you are mature, check your focus. If we don't have a passion for the lost and if we don't have a vision that looks past this life and into the next, God needs to make it clear to us."

Now I am not standing here point a finger at you because I know my own heart and my complacency only too well. Still, I would say that, generally, the Christian church in our society has lost its passion for evangelism. As a young child I remember the salvation army band outside the Royal hotel with the officer pleading with men and women to respond to the gospel. How much now? The church has got a lot to apologise for, the Royal Commission exposed shameful things, but perhaps the church's greatest shame, and its greatest need for apology, is losing its passion for the gospel. Paul in his old age could still weep over the enemies of cross and, to my shame, I have lost that ability. I have been praying that our new pastor, our new general, if I may continue the analogy, will have a burning desire to see souls saved but not just that, be a leader like Paul who can inspire us to strain forward at the task of winning others as we have been won. A man who can teach us to weep over the lost.

When I was young, to encounter an atheist was somewhat rare, I only knew one and he was a sad, morose so and so. Generally, we encountered people who were either believers or at least tolerant of Christianity. Open enemies of the faith lived in other lands and other times but now, in our own blessed country we have become the minority and we are starting to get hints at what might be in store. In verses 18 to 21, the Philippians are reminded that the people they are to reach are enemies of the gospel and are superior in number and probably socially as well, but the believers also needed to be reminded that their enemies end is military disaster.

Though presently hard pressed, the Philippian Christians, who are citizens of heaven, are properly enroled to be eligible for the military rewards that are allocated to members of the campaign. They, just like us, can expect a powerful and able military deliverer, our Lord Jesus Christ, who will allot to them the reward of the transformation of their bodies.

Transition to communion

Just as we see how valued Australian citizenship is to those who will pay large sums and will risk life and limb for the opportunity to gain it, so Roman citizenship was equally valued in ancient times. The commander of the garrison in Jerusalem would say to Paul that he had to pay a great price for his Roman citizenship, a privilege by birth of the Philippian Christians. While we enjoy by right what others strive for, we must also be focused on our true and eternal citizenship, a citizenship purchased at a very great price, the broken body and the shed blood of our Lord Jesus Christ.

Benediction

May the grace of the Lord Jesus Christ, and the love of God, and the fellowship of the Holy Spirit be with you all.

20. PARABLE OF THE SOWER

Reading: Matt 12 30-45

Text Matt 13:1-23 The Parable of the Sower

¹That same day Jesus went out of the house and sat by the lake. ² Such large crowds gathered around him that he got into a boat and sat in it, while all the people stood on the shore. ³ Then he told them many things in parables, saying: "A farmer went out to sow his seed. ⁴ As he was scattering the seed, some fell along the path, and the birds came and ate it up. ⁵ Some fell on rocky places, where it did not have much soil. It sprang up quickly, because the soil was shallow. ⁶ But when the sun came up, the plants were scorched, and they withered because they had no root. ⁷ Other seed fell among thorns, which grew up and choked the plants. ⁸ Still other seed fell on good soil, where it produced a crop—a hundred, sixty or thirty times what was sown. ⁹ Whoever has ears, let them hear."

¹⁰ The disciples came to him and asked, "Why do you speak to the people in parables?"

¹¹ He replied, "Because the knowledge of the secrets of the kingdom of heaven has been given to you, but not to them. ¹² Whoever has will be given more, and they will have an abundance. Whoever does not have, even what they have will be taken from them. ¹³ This is why I speak to them in parables:

"Though seeing, they do not see;
  though hearing, they do not hear or understand.

[14] In them is fulfilled the prophecy of Isaiah:

"'You will be ever hearing but never understanding;
  you will be ever seeing but never perceiving.
[15] For this people's heart has become calloused;
  they hardly hear with their ears,
  and they have closed their eyes.
Otherwise they might see with their eyes,
  hear with their ears,
  understand with their hearts
and turn, and I would heal them.'[a]

[16] But blessed are your eyes because they see, and your ears because they hear. [17] For truly I tell you, many prophets and righteous people longed to see what you see but did not see it, and to hear what you hear but did not hear it.

[18] "Listen then to what the parable of the sower means: [19] When anyone hears the message about the kingdom and does not understand it, the evil one comes and snatches away what was sown in their heart. This is the seed sown along the path. [20] The seed falling on rocky ground refers to someone who hears the word and at once receives it with joy. [21] But since they have no root, they last only a short time. When trouble or persecution comes because of the word, they quickly fall away. [22] The seed falling among the thorns refers to someone who hears the word, but the worries of this life and the deceitfulness of wealth choke the word, making it unfruitful. [23] But the seed falling on good soil refers to someone who hears the word and understands it. This is the one who produces a crop, yielding a hundred, sixty or thirty times what was sown."

I have often said that that if Rachel ever decides to give up money laundering, she could take up a career on the stage. You see, she can make money disappear and can turn a 50 into a 20 before your very eyes. Unfortunately, I am probably at it than her. But I love magic. Not the dark arts of course, but illusion. When you see a good magician at work you just scratch your head and say, however did they do that? You know you are being tricked, sleight of hand, smoke and mirrors, whatever. I love the show *Penn and Teller* when the best magicians from around the world do their tricks in front of these two top Las Vegas magicians and hope that they can do something that stumps even these masters. As much as I respect their ability, they are both ardent atheists and Penn has publicly blasphemed and also denied the existence of the Holy Spirit. He did so believing that he would be crossing a point of no return and so prove that he truly didn't believe in the Biblical God. He was prepared to "accept the consequences" if, or should I say when, after his death he finds that our Lord and saviour does actually exist. He has deliberately intended to place himself outside of the limits of grace.

They were both nominated for membership of the Magic circle in England but were rejected because they had committed the cardinal sin in their eyes, one far greater than attempting to damn their own soul. The motto of the Magic Circle is *indocilis privata loqui*, roughly translated as "not apt to disclose secrets. You never tell the masses how a trick is done and sometimes Penn and Teller would do just that. Hold the thought about the Magic Circle, we are coming back to it.

What a day Jesus had! Our reading just contained a part of it. Until we get to the passion, there is probably no other day recorded in such detail. It starts with Jesus casting out some demons and being accused by the Pharisees and teachers of the Law of being in the Devil's pocket and using the dark arts. They said that the Devil himself, not his minions made his work possible. Jesus reminded them that a kingdom divided cannot stand and tells his critics that there is a limit to grace as blasphemy against the Holy Spirit will not be forgiven. In their behavior they were putting themselves outside the limits of grace, not because the words had magical power to damn their soul but that it exposed the darkness already present in their heart. He told them that you should easily be able to recognize who Christ is by his works but they obstinately refused to believe.

Then the Pharisees and teachers of the law asked him to perform a sign but he chastises them again and no sign will be given other than that of Jonah who was in the fish's belly for 3 days. If the queen of Sheba sought out Solomon to listen to his words surely you should have done the same when a greater than Solomon is here. And that is only by morning tea.

Then his mother and brothers came to take him home because they thought he was going mad and, instead, he owns his disciples. That is, you and I, as his family. Then he went on to the lake and started to teach in parables for apparently the first time. Mark picks up the story in Chapter 4 when they were then caught out in a storm in the lake and Jesus simply commands it to be still. They were terrified and asked each other, "Who is this? Even the wind and the waves obey him!" The wind and waves may obey him but the human heart is another matter.

You all know that I am challenged when it comes to horticulture. If I had turf delivered it would come with a sign "green side up". So, it is a little surprising that I should be introducing a series of sermons based on agricultural parables. But at least you know about good soil. Wikipedia says that the Lockyer Valley has the third most fertile soil in the world.

A prime example of the good soil is just a short distance up the road at Elim, where Tim, our youth pastor and his family live. Years ago, John Windolf told me that at the time there were 12 bores, like the 12 wells at the oasis in Exodus. But I do have an excuse for my brown thumb.

Another Elim is our home opposite Lake Apex, I did not have room for the 70 palms of Exodus so settled on 7. When I was building it, Ray Ferdinand[14] asked if he could drill the post holes with his bobcat. "No worries Ray". There was a worry, he got down 4 inches and could go no further. I had to put down 50 posts 5 feet deep. I have 25 mm of topsoil over mildly decomposed sandstone!! Yes, even I can easily understand the difference between good and bad soil.

But what of the human heart? Back in 1975 when I was training to be a pastor, we were advised to purchase Archbishop Trench's *Notes on the Parables*. An old book, very wordy but very perceptive. The good, soil out text says, or as Luke says, "an honest and a good heart" but the Archbishop asks, "What is this 'honest and good heart'? How can any heart be called good before the Word and the Spirit have made it so? - and yet here the seed finds a good soil and does not make it [good]." And he goes on, explaining "That the heart is good, through receiving the word; not that it receives the word because it is good." The scribes and the Pharisees who saw Jesus' works called good, evil, and said the works of light were the dark arts and could not envisage that they

---

14 A former local mayor and well known businessman.

were at risk of putting themselves outside of the reach of grace. These are the ones who would have claimed to have honest and good hearts. Yet when the light shone they justified themselves while retracted further into their darkness and the Lord took what light they had from them.

The true and honest heart, the good soil that Jesus knows does not belong to those who think they are righteous but those know that they are sinners. To quote the Archbishop again, "who, when the light appeared, did not refuse to be drawn to it, even though they knew that it would condemn their darkness -, that it would require an entire renewing of their hearts, and remodeling of their lives." To quote a much older divine, Augustine, "The beginning of good works is the confession of evil ones". Which one of us here can say. "I cultivated my heart, I made the seed of God's word grow in my heart and by my own strength I will endure to my last breath. The sign of Jonah, three days in the fish, was given to those who believed they held their own salvation in their own hands and demanded a sign. But to those of us who know the need of a saviour will have said with Jonah from the belly of the fish, "Salvation comes from the LORD."

But what of the disciples, what soil were they. [20] But he who received the seed on stony places, this is he who hears the word and immediately receives it with joy; [21] yet he has no root in himself, but endures only for a while. For when tribulation or persecution arises because of the word, immediately he stumbles. Surely this also describes the disciples. Matt 26:31 Then Jesus said to them, "You will all fall away because of Me this night, for it is written, 'I will strike down the shepherd, and the sheep of the flock shall be scattered.' ³² "But after I have been raised, I will go ahead of you to Galilee." ³³ But Peter said to Him, "Even though all may fall away because of You, I will never fall away." ³⁴ Jesus said to him, "Truly I say to you that this very night, before a rooster crows, you will deny Me three times." And yet these were men that had received grace - ¹⁶blessed *are* your eyes for they see, and your ears for they hear; and ¹¹Because it has been given to you to know the mysteries of the kingdom of heaven. Here we have a great mystery, to taste grace, and not just taste it but to eat deeply from it and yet to fall.

We have all seen it and it breaks our heart. Perhaps it was a pastor, perhaps it was a much loved and respected friend, and hardest of all, perhaps it was a family member. What does our parable tell us? Nothing. Parables are not systematic theologies teasing out every last point of detail but broad-brush paintings. What did Jesus say to Peter Luke 22;32 "But I have prayed for you, Simon, that your faith may not fail. And when you have turned back, strengthen your brothers." Let us never, ever forget the merciful saviour that, when a man seems to go beyond the reach of grace, restores that which was lost, a saviour who can take the wheat planted in stony ground and transplant it in the good soil. What do you do if you have a patch of ground that isn't producing properly? Sell it off to your neighbour and hope he doesn't know he is being sold a pup. Or do you work that soil with all your skill and restore it. If we, who are in need of a savior, know how to do that how much more will your heavenly father work in the hearts of those we love. Those for whom we ask no more that the same grace be shown to them as was shown to us.

When I was a young man training to be a pastor, every Sunday I would get up at 5.00, even in the middle of winter to travel to a little Baptist chapel. Initially it was to meet a young lady but later because of the strong friendship that developed between the pastor and myself. Twice I got to hear a visiting lay preacher, Frank Hamford, but he was like no lay preacher I had ever heard before or since. He had a presence and eloquence in the pulpit that few professionals possess. When he spoke, and from the examples he used, you knew this was an educated and cultured man. I remember him 44 years on. My friend told me his story. He was a Baptist pastor in Hastings back in about 1936 but he fell away and left his wife for another woman and had four children by her. Bad enough now but imagine the scandal then! There was no simple divorce in those days and there never was one. Frank became a magician, and a very good magician at that and rose high in the magic circle even performing for the king.

What soil was that that the seed was planted in? Was this a man that had put himself beyond the reach of grace, having tasted deeply of it and yet turning his back on it? But in 1959 one of his sons was converted, from his wife or common law wife I don't know which, but Frank went to his baptism. There the Lord brought the magician under conviction and restored him never to fall again. He never did return to magic. He wrote a biography, *A Brand Snatched from the Burning* yet, my friends, every one of us here is a brand snatched from the burning.

So, what do I want you take from this sermon this morning? In a word it is "restitution". The Parable of the Sower was spoken to men who would fail and fail very spectacularly. But they could not escape grace and the one who strengthened them was the one who denied Jesus three times with an oath. My friends, it is only grace that drew us and it is only grace that holds us, not some goodness possessed in our heart that made us worthy of our Lord's mercy. This mercy that we received must give us confidence to ask that the same mercy be extended to those we love, many of whom have tasted of God's grace and yet turned their backs on him. They may not have intentionally blasphemed and they may not have deliberately sinned against the Holy Spirit but, none the less, they are living in the far country as another parable described it. The context of this parable will not let us say, "They are beyond grace because the soil is bad." God only saves sinners and his promise to those of us who he has given much is that more will be given.

21. NO OTHER NAME

Gatton and Tenthill Baptist church were on camp together and at the last moment was asked to deliver a sermon to the "stragglers" in Gatton. Pastor Doug had started a series on Acts and I was given the first half of Chapter 4 to base my message on. It was also the 500th anniversary of the Reformation.

Reading: Acts 4 The priests and the captain of the temple guard and the Sadducees came up to Peter and John while they were speaking to the people. ^{2} They were greatly disturbed because the apostles were teaching the people, proclaiming in Jesus the resurrection of the dead. ^{3} They seized Peter and John and, because it was evening, they put them in jail until the next day. ^{4} But many who heard the message believed; so the number of men who believed grew to about five thousand.

^{5} The next day the rulers, the elders and the teachers of the law met in Jerusalem. ^{6} Annas the high priest was there, and so were Caiaphas, John, Alexander and others of the high priest's family. ^{7} They had Peter and John brought before them and began to question them: "By what power or what name did you do this?"

^{8} Then Peter, filled with the Holy Spirit, said to them: "Rulers and elders of the people! ^{9} If we are being called to account today for an act of kindness shown to a man who was lame and are being asked how he was healed, ^{10} then know this, you and all the people of Israel: It is by the name of Jesus Christ of Nazareth, whom you crucified but whom God raised from the dead, that this man stands before you healed. ^{11} Jesus is

"'the stone you builders rejected,
  which has become the cornerstone.'

^{12} Salvation is found in no one else, for there is no other name under heaven given to mankind by which we must be saved."

¹³ When they saw the courage of Peter and John and realized that they were unschooled, ordinary men, they were astonished and they took note that these men had been with Jesus. ¹⁴ But since they could see the man who had been healed standing there with them, there was nothing they could say. ¹⁵ So they ordered them to withdraw from the Sanhedrin and then conferred together. ¹⁶ "What are we going to do with these men?" they asked. "Everyone living in Jerusalem knows they have performed a notable sign, and we cannot deny it. ¹⁷ But to stop this thing from spreading any further among the people, we must warn them to speak no longer to anyone in this name."

¹⁸ Then they called them in again and commanded them not to speak or teach at all in the name of Jesus. ¹⁹ But Peter and John replied, "Which is right in God's eyes: to listen to you, or to him? You be the judges! ²⁰ As for us, we cannot help speaking about what we have seen and heard."

²¹ After further threats they let them go. They could not decide how to punish them, because all the people were praising God for what had happened. ²² For the man who was miraculously healed was over forty years old.

> Acts 4:12 Salvation is found in no one else, for there is no other name under heaven given to mankind by which we must be saved.

Text: Acts 4:12 Salvation is found in no one else, for there is no other name under heaven given to mankind by which we must be saved."

Introduction

Amazon is coming to Australia.

We hear a lot about what the digital disruption is already doing worldwide and probably no part of the economy may be harder hit than the family business. In our reading we see another family business and what they were selling was God. But you know, to be in business you must have, first of all, a product and you must believe in what you are selling. What kind of a God were they selling, and selling was the operative word as they had turned the temple into a den of thieves. For example, only animals they approved could be sacrificed and they did this at vastly inflated prices and charged half a day's wages just to give change.

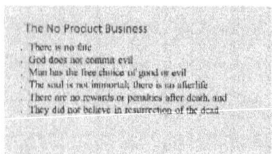

But they were a business without a product! The Sadducees believed that:

- There is no fate
- God does not commit evil
- Man has the free choice of good or evil
- The soul is not immortal; there is no afterlife
- There are no rewards or penalties after death, and

- They did not believe in resurrection of the dead

Drop the second item and you could be describing the secular world today. This group, which made up the upper social and economic echelon of Judean society, controlled every aspect of its funds and government and foreign relations again, much like our own government except they also had the keys to the temple and attempted to control how people worshipped and what it was acceptable to believe and say and do. We will find, with this same sex marriage bill that many in our government will want to go there too. The family business run by the Sadducees was about to be rocked by a disruption far greater than Amazon ever will be - the gospel of Jesus Christ. Do you believe it is as disruptive now as it was then? I certainly do.

When Jesus was alive the "Business" said that his works were only possible because the very Devil himself empowered God's beloved son. But he was easily gotten rid of and discredited when they had the Romans crucify him. Every Jew knew the significance of that. Moses had written "you must not leave the body hanging on the pole overnight. Be sure to bury it that same day, because anyone who is hung on a pole is under God's curse" (Dt 21:23). Cursed with the penalty of your sin and mine that he bore on the hill of Golgotha. They remembered, when the disciples didn't, that Jesus had said he would rise on the third day, a preposterous idea when there is only oblivion beyond the grave, but they set a guard on the tomb to ensure the body could not be stolen by the disciples.

Sadducees buying the guards' silence

Now, that didn't go as expected as they had to pay a large amount of money to keep the guards silent who were witnesses to the angels and the resurrection. To make matters worse, the dead man's disciples are now preaching that he is alive and gathering followers by the thousand.

Peter and John before the Sanhedrin

Standing before them was not just Peter and John but also a man they had known for many years as a cripple. They had probably thrown him a few coins to make them feel good about themselves but now he stood before them whole. This was something they couldn't deny as it was too public and how could they put this down to the Devil when everyone was praising God because of it. Intimidation was all they had. Whose name did you use. Abraham, Moses, Elijah, or do you dare to mention the name of the cursed and crucified heretic? Say the word "Jesus" and risk the same penalty as your crucified carpenter. But Peter and John had been with Jesus. They had denied him and deserted him on the night of his arrest, but Jesus had sought them out, restored them and filled them with his Spirit. Jesus had promised them "When you are brought before synagogues, rulers and authorities, do not worry about how you will defend yourselves or what you will say, [12] for the Holy Spirit will teach you at that time what you should say". The Lord was faithful to Peter and John as he is to us, "know this, you and all the people of Israel: It is by the name of Jesus Christ of

Nazareth, whom you crucified but whom God raised from the dead, that this man stands before you healed. Salvation is found in no one else, for there is no other name under heaven given to mankind by which we must be saved" (Luke 12:11-12). May the same Spirit teach us also to say, "Amen".

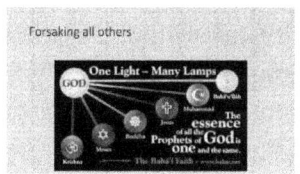

This was as much an anathema to them then as it is today, and they did everything in their power to deny men the salvation of their eternal souls. Your soul is immortal, but unless you are trusting Jesus it is not one with him and it must be redeemed. Salvation is not an optional extra to pick up or discard without consequence. There isn't one god with many messengers. Salvation is found in no one else. It is exclusive, as must be our response, using the words of the marriage vow, "forsaking all others." Exclusive it may be, but it doesn't exclude because the gospel invites all to join. But what is this salvation? I can tell you what it is now, if I had to put the gospel in 10 words or less it is "God's gracious offer of forgiveness in Christ Jesus." For today it is friendship with your maker and a brother that will walk beside you every day. But we will die and there is no oblivion as the Sadducees proclaimed, but we will rise again. Jesus' own resurrection assures us of that, but what then? I can't say much. Paul even struggled with what to say "However, as it is written: "What no eye has seen, what no ear has heard, and what no human mind has conceived" -- the things God has prepared for those who love him"" (1 Cor 2;9).

Fast forward 1500 years and the Sadducees had been long relegated to history. Since then the declaration of salvation being found only in Jesus had become mired in years of tradition, error, unbelief and very dark behaviour by some. Yet, side by side, from others, there was courage, and a struggle to know the truth and be faithful to the light they have received. Concerning that long tradition, Baptists generally don't give much time to the Christian calendar except for the two biggies, Christmas and Easter. We also tend to get a warm and fuzzy about a fairly recent innovation, Mother's Day but things like Harvest Sunday and saints feast days don't get a look in. That is just who we are as Baptists. But today is a biggie in the church calendar. It is Reformation Sunday and not just another year rolling around. 500 years ago, on the evening of October 31st, Martin Luther nailed his 95 Theses on the door of the castle church door at Wittenberg, a date which is generally considered to be the start of a revolution whereby we are free to believe or disbelieve whatever we want when it comes to our maker. Free to choose maybe, but not free of the consequences of that choice to taste or reject that salvation found in no other name.

500 years ago, Pope Leo 10th was building St Peter Basilica in Rome and needed money, and lots of it. How do you do this? His answer was to sell what was called indulgences, your get out of jail card. These indulgences, it was claimed, would free you from both the guilt and punishment of sins previously committed and from sins yet to be committed. But it wasn't only for the living but for your deceased loved ones. Unlike the Sadducees business model, they did not want to deny salvation to the masses, they were in the

business of selling forgiveness and would say of those who may have lived like devils:

As soon as the gold in the casket rings
The rescued soul to heaven springs

The 95 Theses was a call by Luther for a theological debate about the scriptural validity of the business of selling salvation. There was no way of knowing where this was heading but it had never ended well in the past for those who rocked the boat and intimidation had been a very effective way of silencing dissent. The battle lines became drawn over what Luther saw as a periphery issue; the real battle was salvation by faith. There was no doubt in Luther's mind that Salvation is found in no one else, for there is no other name under heaven given to mankind by which we must be saved. He would set off a disruption, the benefits of which we, believers and unbelievers alike now take for granted every day.

Foundation Stone

Move forward 500 years. The significance of the reformation used to be taught in schools but I don't suppose it is now and nobody cares about what great cost in suffering, blood and smoke it was be a protestant and a Baptist in particular, or even dare I say and agnostic or an atheist. Our society that owes its prosperity and freedom to the Christian gospel is rapidly turning its back on the source of its favour. It was the cornerstone on which everything was measured. Now there are forces at work that can only be seen as diabolical in the true sense of the word. I hardly need to elaborate them as your heart should be as grieved as mine is over them. We read with horror of Herod and the slaughter of the innocents in Bethlehem. Yet there is all but silence about the approximately 80,000 abortions annually in Australia and material taught to children in our schools under the Safe Schools program is classed as MA15+ for the rest of and only available after 8.30 pm. The list of godless innovations grows day by day.

Christianity is seditious, make no mistake about it. It has rejected vehemently the dictates of others to not speak the truth, whether it be Jewish religious leaders, roman emperors and corrupt religious systems, even if it calls itself Christian. The true faith doesn't just roll over when it is told to be quiet and there are times when a Christian must stand and declare, "Salvation is found in no one else, for there is no other name under heaven given to mankind by which we must be saved." Let me quote another writer, "The true gospel must be fought for in every generation. Likewise, in every generation, there will be an attack on God's Word and biblical preaching. We see these things in our day, and the Church is called to stand and be the light in the midst of darkness. Learning from faithful servants who have gone before us can help prepare and equip us." Obeying God rather than man in the road ahead may require some difficult choices, some small, some large. As an example, the wife of a friend is a florist but she has closed her business rather than be, forced to provide flowers for same sex marriages.

Conclusion

James and John had neither silver or gold but only the name by which we must be saved. In their day, the threats of the Godless religious powers could not stop the Gospels advance and men were reconciled by no other name but Jesus. Luther owned nothing, and his monks cowl was worn out and had asked for charity to purchase another. In that worn out garment he dared take a hopeless stand against Rome. "My mind is made captive by the word of God I am bound by the scriptures adduced." Today, the church itself seems to be worn out, weak and discredited in large part by those in leadership who had betrayed their Lord and those in their charge and by others who offer no more religion than the Sadducees, religion without exclusivity, substance or hope. Yes there is going to be a battle for the gospel and their remains no other name that can save individuals and nations. Is the church too weak for this challenge?

When writing my book "Pain and a Powerful God" I read the account by the German preacher Helmut Thielicke when he was in a gestapo prison . He earned the right to be listened to. He told in one of his books a story that shat should give us hope as we contemplate the future of the Gospel. "As a young pastor in Nazi Germany, he was determined to appropriate Jesus' statement, "All power is given me in heaven and earth." In the nation at that time, Adolf Hitler held sway, but the young Thielicke repeated in his mind Christ's audacious words. He thereby assured himself that Hitler and his dreadful Nazi machine "were merely puppets hanging by strings in the hands of the mighty Lord." At his first

Bible study, however, he found himself facing two old ladies and a still older organist with palsied fingers. Was this what the Lord with all power in heaven and earth was about? Outside marched battalions of brown shits who were subject to totally different lords. That evening, he wondered what God offered. Didn't this "utterly miserable response" refute Jesus' declaration? He compared his feelings that evening to those of the disciples when Jesus announced his coming Kingdom. They knew the Romans still occupied the seats of power." Where are the Sadducees, where are the Romans, where even are the brown shirts?

> Acts 4:12 Salvation is found in no one else, for there is no other name under heaven given to mankind by which we must be saved.

There is salvation in no other name.

ABOUT THE AUTHOR

Edgar Stubbersfield (known as Ted) grew up in the small town of Gatton in Queensland, Australia in the 50's. It was a good time to be young. Life was simple, relatively safe and faith in God was taken for granted. After being thrown out of school in 1965 he started an apprenticeship as a motor mechanic, something he was ill suited to. In 1970, Ted went on an extended trip overseas and was confronted by the Christian gospel in many countries and saw for the first time that there was a God who was alive. That year he met with Jesus in a Damascus road type experience.

Ministry seemed to be the logical call on his life and he trained initially with the Church of Christ and then in the UK with the Elim Pentecostal Church but found himself most at home with a remarkable group of Grace Baptists. The Lord had mercy on His church and Ted went back to the family business, a sawmill. He kept his interest in Christian faith, living and doctrine by studying by correspondence and by writing. He completed a Master of Theology in Applied Theology in 2011 through the University of Wales.

Ted has a number of other publications but in a very different field, weather exposed timber structures. He is currently working as a consultant in this field.

www.ingramcontent.com/pod-product-compliance
Lightning Source LLC
Chambersburg PA
CBHW071457040426
42444CB00008B/1377